The God of all comfort

Reflections in the book of Isaiah

Roger Ellsworth

EVANGELICAL PRESS

EVANGELICAL PRESS
Faverdale North Industrial Estate, Darlington, DL3 0PH,
England

Evangelical Press USA
P. O. Box 825, Webster, New York 14580, USA

e-mail: sales@evangelicalpress.org
web: www.evangelicalpress.org

First published 2004

British Library Cataloguing in Publication Data available

ISBN 0 85234 549 6

Printed and bound in Great Britain by Creative Print and
Design Wales, Ebbw Vale, South Wales.

The God of all comfort

The following pages are dedicated to Dr LaVerne Butler and Dr Paige Patterson

Acknowledgements

I again find myself indebted to many for making these pages possible. My heartfelt thanks go Immanuel Baptist Church for faithfully and joyfully listening to the sermons from which this book was born. Thanks also to my wife Sylvia and to my secretary Laura Simmons for their kind assistance. As always, I am profoundly grateful to the editors of Evangelical Press.

May God be pleased to use these chapters to bring comfort to many troubled hearts!

Contents

Introduction

The prophecy of Isaiah consists of sixty-six chapters, of which the last twenty-seven chapters may be considered to be a book within a book. These chapters, which are bound together by the theme of comfort, could be called 'God's Book of Comfort'. This section begins with the prophet relating the command he had received from the Lord:

> 'Comfort, yes, comfort my people!'
> Says your God.
> 'Speak comfort to Jerusalem…'

As we look at the succeeding chapters, we find that Isaiah did as he was commanded. His words fairly brim with comfort and encouragement.

How encouraging these chapters must have been to their first readers! They would sorely need all the comfort Isaiah could provide. Who were these people? They were citizens of Judah who had seen their nation and their city of Jerusalem, with its beautiful temple, destroyed by the Babylonians. They would read these words from Babylon itself where they would spend seventy long years of captivity.

They would often find their faith failing and their spirits flagging during those years. Had God forgotten them? Were his promises still in effect? What lay ahead of them?

Enabled by the Spirit of God to see what his people would be going through in Babylon, Isaiah was able to answer all these questions and others as well.

Things today are both different and the same. While God's people find their circumstances to be quite different from those of Isaiah's original readers, we find ourselves asking their questions. The answers of Isaiah still apply, answers that bring as much comfort to us as they did for those people long ago.

We need this comfort, but, alas, many of us are deprived of it because this portion of the Word of God seems in many places to be strange and hard to understand. It is my prayer that the following chapters will provide double help, that they will clear up some of the mystery and will draw out some of the comfort.

This section of God's Word seems to lend itself quite well to a devotional format, and this book has been structured in that way. The beginning of each chapter contains some suggestions on how to make the most of the text that follows. Each chapter ends with some questions that are intended to encourage the reader to preserve some of his or her thoughts in journal form. This is a wonderfully helpful discipline, and I hope this book will be instrumental in encouraging some to start and others to continue.

Approached in this way, the reader will have devotional material for twenty-seven days, and, I pray, increasing adoration for and faith in our glorious God.

Come along with me now as we visit each of these precious, comforting chapters in the Word of our God.

Isaiah 40:10-11

Behold, the Lord GOD shall come with a strong hand,
And his arm shall rule for him;
Behold, his reward is with him,
And his work before him.
He will feed his flock like a shepherd;
He will gather the lambs with his arm,
And carry them in his bosom,
And gently lead those who are with young.

Day 1
Our deliverer and shepherd

- *Begin by reading Isaiah 40*
- *Pray about what you have read*
- *Make notes on what you think God is teaching you*
- *Read the following chapter*
- *Answer the questions in the section 'For your journal'*

Isaiah 40:10-11

The prophecy of Isaiah falls into two major sections. The first section (chapters 1 - 39) deals with events in Judah during Isaiah's life. This section features the prophet calling his people to repent of their sins and warning them that they will be taken captive in Babylon if they refuse to do so.

In the second section (chapters 40 - 66), the prophet looks beyond his own time and the impending captivity of his people to the end of that captivity and their restoration to their own land. Because these chapters talk about the future, some have argued that Isaiah could not have written them. This view assumes that God could not have given Isaiah a preview of the future. It goes without saying that God, who is unlimited in power and wisdom, was perfectly able to do so.

Furthermore, it is altogether reasonable to believe he would do so. Matthew Henry writes: 'Before God sent his people into captivity he furnished them with precious promises for their support and comfort in their trouble; and we may well imagine of what great use to them the glorious, gracious light of this prophecy was in that cloudy and dark day, and how much it helped to dry up their tears by the rivers of Babylon.'[1]

We look at this portion of Isaiah's prophecy because we stand as much in need of comfort as those ancient captives in Babylon. As they experienced despondency and depression over their circumstances, so do many of God's people today. As many of them faced the pressure of trying to be faithful in the midst of a hostile culture, so do many saints today. As many of them nurtured doubts about whether God's promises regarding them would be fulfilled, so many Christians today struggle with questions and doubts.

Time spent in these latter chapters of Isaiah looking for comfort is time well spent. Encouragement and consolation abound here, so much so that we will only attempt to study some of the comforting verses in these chapters.

The verses before us are sweet indeed. They present us with two awe-inspiring pictures of God.

The mighty deliverer

Isaiah says:

> Behold, the Lord GOD shall come with a strong hand,
> And his arm shall rule for him;
> Behold, his reward is with him,
> And his work before him
>
> (v. 10).

With these words, Isaiah assured the people of Judah that captivity in Babylon would not be their final state. The Lord would come to them and deliver them.

That promise probably seemed too good to be true to the captive Jews. Their Babylonian captors were so very strong. Was it reasonable to expect deliverance? Isaiah's words make it clear that deliverance from captivity was not a matter of Babylon's strength but rather God's strength.

When God came to effect the deliverance of his people, the outcome would not be in doubt. God would come 'with a strong hand' and his arm would 'rule' or 'prevail' for him. In other words, God's strong arm would be sufficient for him to prevail over any foe that would seek to prevent the deliverance.

The phrase 'his reward is with him' is yet another indication of God's strength. His reward was the restoration of his people to their land. Isaiah pictures God carrying that reward in his strong arms, and the implication is that no one could wrest that blessing out of those arms. It was a blessing God was carrying to his people, and it would be delivered to them without fail. The following phrase 'And his work before him' is another way of saying the same thing. God's work or 'recompense' is the same as his reward. It is his work of deliverance and restoration, a work which would most certainly be achieved.

The deliverance of God's people from their captivity in Babylon cannot begin to compare with a far greater deliverance each and every child of God has experienced; that is, deliverance from sin and condemnation.

Make no mistake about it, that deliverance is the result of our mighty God working on our behalf. No one can take a shred of credit for himself on this matter of salvation. It is all God's doing. He, the mighty deliverer, planned our redemption before the world began; then, in the fulness of time, he sent his Son, Jesus Christ, to work it out. The Lord Jesus did this by going to the cross where he defeated Satan and purchased our salvation, a salvation which was power-fully applied to us by the Holy Spirit as he opened our blind eyes, broke down our stubborn resistance to the gospel and gave us life.

That brings us to the second picture of God in these verses.

The caring Shepherd

Isaiah says:

> He will feed his flock like a shepherd;
> He will gather the lambs with his arm,
> And carry them in his bosom,
> And gently lead those who are with young
>
> (v. 11).

The Hebrew word translated 'feed' means more than merely supplying food. Albert Barnes writes: 'It refers to all the care of a shepherd over his flock; and means to tend, to guard, to govern, to provide pasture, to defend from danger, as a shep-herd does his flock.'[2]

With these words, then, Isaiah was promising his people that in addition to delivering them, God would shepherd them. The same God who would deliver them by crushing their foes would be tender with his own people. He would not deal with them as a fierce conqueror, but rather as a shepherd caring for his sheep.

He is the self-existing, uncreated and eternal Lord, whose love and care, whose providence and power, are all unlimited and inexhaustible. Who, then, can deny that He is an All-sufficient Shepherd? In strength He is almighty; in wisdom, omniscient; in love, unequalled; in resources, unbounded! What are those evils which He cannot foresee? What is that danger which He cannot avert? Where is that enemy whom He cannot subdue? What is the name or nature of that want which He is unable to supply? The various members of His flock are as different in their age, their dispositions, and their temptations, as they are in their language, their country, and their race; and yet, the eye of the Jehovah-Shepherd observes each of His widely scattered sheep as minutely as if they were all gathered before Him at one place, and His ear is as open to their various requests as if He had only to regard the voice of a single petitioner. Indeed, His hand can administer out of the fulness of His merits, to each and all of them at any and every moment, those blessings which will prove most suitable to their case.

Joel R. Beeke, Jehovah Shepherding His Sheep[3]

Isaiah's words about God's shepherdly care of his people must have come as a great consolation to the captives in Babylon. The very God against whom their nation had so grievously sinned had a mild and tender disposition towards them. This tenderness is displayed again and again in the closing chapters of Isaiah. Later we find the Lord himself saying:

'For a mere moment I have forsaken you,
But with great mercies I will gather you.
With a little wrath I hid my face from you for a moment;
But with everlasting kindness I will have mercy on you'
(54:7-8).

As we ponder Isaiah's words further, we cannot help but note that it extends even to the very weakest, the lambs and those with young. While God shows tenderness to all his people, he is especially tender towards the young and the needy in his flock.

What encouragement these verses provide God's people today! God has not changed one iota in how he looks upon them. They are as much the objects of his tender care now as they were centuries ago.

Conscious of our many weaknesses and failings, we easily fall into the habit of thinking of God as the gigantic police-man in the skies who is always angry with his people and ever ready to bash them with his celestial truncheon. Of course, the Bible does indeed teach that God regards sin seriously and finds it necessary to chastise his children; but he does so out of a heart of love and with great tenderness.

If we doubt the tenderness of God towards his people, we only have to look at the Lord Jesus Christ who said, 'I am the good shepherd. The good shepherd gives his life for the sheep' (John 10:11). And give his life he did. On the cross, the Lord Jesus Christ purchased his flock. And now he feeds, defends and leads them.

What, dear believer, is causing your heart to ache? What is it that burdens and troubles you? Are you despondent over a set of circumstances that seem beyond your control? Are you burdened by guilt over a glaring failure to live for God? The devil will be quick to tell you that God wants nothing at all to do with you. But the cross of Calvary tells you that those same strong arms that delivered you from sin and made you God's child are there to carry you in shepherdly compassion and love. You need never doubt God's love for you. He has demon-strated it once and for all on that cross. And you may rest in that love even while you are troubled. God, your shepherd, knows about your trouble. He knows the ache of your heart. And he knows the purposes that he has for you. He has your best interest at heart in every situation of life and is sustaining you and helping you even when you feel that he has utterly forgotten you.

Young Christian, you face many trials, temptations and snares. It may seem to you that no one understands or cares. I tell you now that the Christ who loved you and died for you has a special concern for you. He knows your temptations and your feebleness, and, even when you seem completely alone, he is with you to carry you along and help you.

What a God we have! Mighty to deliver! Tender in disposition! How very eager we should be to live for him!

For your journal...

1. Do you find yourself constantly battling discouragement in your Christian walk? Can you identify the things that cause you to be discouraged?

2. Do you find comfort in thinking of God as your deliverer? Check your concordance for other Scriptures that present God in this way. Study in particular Colossians 1:9-14. Write down truths this passage teaches about God delivering his people.

3. Does the picture of God as shepherd comfort you? Does this picture make you think of Psalm 23? Read this psalm. What does it teach about God's shepherdly care?

Isaiah 41:8-10, 14

'But you, Israel, are my servant,
Jacob whom I have chosen,
The descendants of Abraham my friend.
You whom I have taken from the ends of the earth,
And called from its farthest regions,
And said to you,
"You are my servant,
I have chosen you and have not cast you away:
Fear not, for I am with you;
Be not dismayed, for I am your God.
I will strengthen you,
Yes, I will help you,
I will uphold you with my righteous right hand."

...

'Fear not, you worm Jacob,
You men of Israel!
I will help you,' says the LORD
And your Redeemer, the Holy One of Israel.

Day 2
Unbreakable cords of comfort

♦ *Begin by reading Isaiah 41*
♦ *Pray about what you have read*
♦ *Make notes on what you think God is teaching you*
♦ *Read the following chapter*
♦ *Answer the questions in the section 'For your journal'*

Isaiah 41:8-10, 14

As we consider this passage we must ever keep in mind that the prophet's message was originally intended for people who were in captivity in Babylon. We can only very imperfectly imagine what a severe trial this was. They had been torn away from everything they held near and dear, everything that was familiar and comforting, and they lived with a great amount of fear and uncertainty about the future. The Babylonians were so very strong, and they, the Jews, were so very weak and feeble. It must often have seemed to them that their future was limited to Babylon.

In the verses before us, the Lord graciously addresses their fear. He says 'Fear not' three times in the space of five verses (vv. 10, 13, 14). In verse 10, he says, 'Be not dismayed'. The word 'dismayed' means, in the words of Albert Barnes, 'to look about as one does in a state of alarm, or danger'.[1]

We should note that the Lord was not content merely to say, 'Fear not'. He proceeded to give his people reasons why they should not be afraid. These reasons are wrapped up in the phrases 'I have', 'I am' and 'I will'. We can think of these as three unbreakable cords of comfort.

'I have'

First, the Lord says to his trembling people that their fears are unfounded because of something he had already done (vv. 8-9). He says, 'I have chosen' the descendants of Abraham.

These must have come as welcome words to the captives in Babylon. Their circumstances were such that it must have seemed to them that they had no relationship with God at all, that he cared nothing for them, that they were really no different from all the other nations. But God assured them that there was a huge difference between the other nations and themselves.

That difference was about to become very clear indeed. The first seven verses of this forty-first chapter consist of God's ringing call to the nations to prepare themselves for his destructive wrath. But this wrath would not come upon God's people because he had placed his love upon them and called them to himself.

Yes, God's people were in captivity in Babylon because of God's judgement. But even that judgement was different. It was temporary chastisement out of a heart of love, rather than complete destruction out of anger and fury. The latter will never be experienced by those who truly belong to the Lord.

Ours is a day in which the people of God are treated increasingly with disdain and contempt. Our pagan society is ever quick to assure us that there is nothing to our faith, that we do not stand in a special covenant relationship with God, and that our claim to that end constitutes insufferable dogmatism and arrogance. The climate of our society is such that it is very easy for Christians to feel fearful and doubtful.

Against the multitude of voices that make us afraid is the calm assurance of our God that we are indeed his. We are his, not because of any merit of our own, but rather because of his grace. We are his because he graciously chose us for himself and called us unto himself.

> *The apostle Paul emphasized God's choice or election of his people with these words: '...he chose us in him before the foundation of the world, that we should be holy and without blame before him in love, having predestined us to adoption as sons by Jesus Christ to himself, according to the good pleasure of his will, to the praise of the glory of his grace, by which he made us accepted in the Beloved' (Eph. 1:4-6).*
>
> *In those verses we have:*
>
> - *the fact of election — 'he chose us' (v. 4)*
> - *the time — 'before the foundation of the world' (v. 4)*
> - *the basis — 'according to the good pleasure of his will' (v. 5)*
> - *the instrument — 'in him', that is, in Christ (v. 4)*
> - *the purposes — 'that we should be holy and without blame before him in love' (v. 4); 'to the praise of the glory of his grace' (v. 6).*

This doctrine should fill us with humility and gratitude. Those who are saved owe it all to God, who chose them for himself,

paid for their sins in Christ and enabled them to receive the
Lord Jesus Christ as their Saviour.

Some profess to be alarmed by such teaching. The truth is
that there is nothing more comforting. If salvation in any way
depended on us, we would have cause to worry. But since God
has taken upon himself the whole of the work, we can rest
and rejoice in him.

'I am'

That brings us to the second reason the Lord told his people
not to fear, namely, because of those things that were pres-
ently true (v. 10). Twice in this verse the Lord uses the words
'I am'.

'I am with you'

Multitudes of Christians have testified that nothing is more
precious to them than knowing that the Lord is with them.
He is there to sympathize and to understand. We feel we can
face almost anything as long as we do not have to face it alone.

But what about those times when we do not feel the presence of God? Most Christians would say there are many such
times. God has promised never to leave us nor forsake us, but
sometimes it feels as if he has. The glad answer from Scripture
is that the Lord is present even when it seems he is not. He is
there to strengthen and help us even if it appears he has abandoned us.

Think for a moment about the life of Joseph. He must have
felt forsaken by God when he was sold by his brothers into

slavery. He must have felt the same when he was unjustly cast
into prison. But years later, he was able to look back and see
the hand of God in it all. He said to his brothers, '...you meant
evil against me; but God meant it for good...' (Gen. 50:20).
Joseph teaches us not to pronounce on what God is doing in
our lives until all the evidence is in.

The Lord then uses another 'I am' phrase in this verse.

'I am your God'

What a consolation this was for those captive Jews! They were
in captivity because they had sinned against the Lord and he
had used Babylon as his instrument of judgement. The captivity must have made those Jews think that God was so thoroughly ashamed of them that he would have nothing more to
do with them. But God had not cast them off. They were still
his people, and he was still their God.

If we ever come to know God, we can never get away from
him. He is our God by covenant. He has pledged himself to us
in grace, and his grace will win out over all our sins and failures so that we can triumphantly say with Paul: '...we are
more than conquerors through him who loved us' and nothing
'shall be able to separate us from the love of God which is in
Christ Jesus our Lord' (Rom. 8:37, 39).

'I will'

The third reason the captives were not to fear relates to that
which the Lord promised for the future.

The Lord says:

'I will strengthen you,
Yes, I will help you.
I will uphold you with my righteous right hand'

(v. 10).

Alan Redpath calls Isaiah 41 'the great I WILL chapter of the
Bible'. Fourteen times in this chapter the Lord says 'I will'.
Redpath says, 'When God says "I will," He says it with all the
authority of omnipotence. He has foreseen every difficulty.
He has studied every obstacle which may come in His way. He
has anticipated every possible contingency. He knows the
weakness of the one to whom He makes His promise, and yet
He says "I will!"'[2]

With the words of verse 10, the Lord promises to provide
the captives with all the strength and help they would need
for the challenges of the future. They would be released from
their captivity, but that would not be the end of their difficulties. A long, dangerous journey from Babylon to Jerusalem
would confront them. And after that there was the daunting
task of rebuilding their homes, their cities and the temple.

Such challenges were enough to make them shrink in dis-
may. But those challenges could and would be met because
the Lord pledged himself to help and uphold them. He would
enable them every step of the way. He was more than adequate
for every situation. We do not have to be strong when the
Lord is strong on our behalf.

We surely cannot read these instances of God saying 'I will'
without looking beyond this life and its difficulties to the very
end. Yes, God has promised to help and strengthen us in this
life, but he has also given us a glorious 'I will' regarding what
lies beyond this life. He says he will raise our bodies from the
grave to share in his eternal glory (1 Thess. 4:13-18).

This forty-first chapter of Isaiah gives us reason to rejoice. In the midst of our burdens and heartaches, the Lord speaks to us. He says 'I have', 'I am' and 'I will'. He says we are his because of what he has done in the past. He says he is with us now as a very present help in time of trouble. He says he will be all we need in the future, in what remains of this life and in the life to come.

How do we know all this is true? Is it just wishful thinking? No, it is far more solid than that. Look to the Lord Jesus Christ. He left the glories of heaven behind and came to this earth to endure incredible hardship. He died a special death on the cross of Calvary, where he actually endured the wrath of God in our place.

Now, brothers and sisters in Christ, here is inescapable logic. If God would go so far to save us from our sins, we should never doubt his love for us and his pledge to strengthen and help us.

You see, everything else God has pledged to do for us is less than that which he has already done. If he was willing to do the most for us, namely, punishing his Son in our place, we may rest assured that he will never fail to do less, that is, strengthen us and help us.

For your journal...

1. Write down additional Scriptures that use the phrase 'Fear not'. How do these passages comfort you?

2. Locate other Scriptures in which God says, 'I am'. How do these passages help you?

3. Do you find comfort in the doctrine of election? Write down
   specific ways in which this doctrine provides comfort.

4. Try to find other passages in which God says 'I will'. Write
   down the specific promises God makes in these passages.

Isaiah 42:1-6

'Behold! My Servant whom I uphold,
My Elect One in whom my soul delights!
I have put my Spirit upon him;
He will bring forth justice to the Gentiles.
He will not cry out, nor raise his voice,
Nor cause his voice to be heard in the street.
A bruised reed he will not break,
And smoking flax he will not quench;
He will bring forth justice for truth.
He will not fail nor be discouraged,
Till he has established justice in the earth;
And the coastlands shall wait for his law.'

Thus says God the LORD,
Who created the heavens and stretched them out,
Who spread forth the earth and that which comes from it,
Who gives breath to the people on it,
And spirit to those who walk on it:
'I, the LORD, have called you in righteousness,
And will hold your hand;
I will keep you and give you as a covenant to the people,
As a light to the Gentiles…'

Day 3
The comforting Christ

- ♦ *Begin by reading Isaiah 42*
- ♦ *Pray about what you have read*
- ♦ *Make notes on what you think God is teaching you*
- ♦ *Read the following chapter*
- ♦ *Answer the questions in the section 'For your journal'*

Isaiah 42:1-6

The latter chapters of Isaiah contain several references to the Servant of the Lord. We get into difficulty if we insist on identifying this servant in only one way. In some passages, the term refers to the nation of Israel; in others, it refers to the Messiah.

In the above verses, it is obvious that the reference is to the Messiah. This is borne out by the Gospel of Matthew, which specifically affirms that Jesus was the fulfilment of these verses (Matt. 12:16-21).

We recall that this portion of Isaiah's prophecy was written to provide comfort for the Jewish captives in Babylon. In the light of that, we might very well find ourselves wondering why

Isaiah would include a prophecy about the coming Messiah. How would this provide comfort for those captives? Albert Barnes answers in this way: '...the design of the Spirit here in introducing this reference to the Messiah is, to comfort the hearts of the exile Jews with the assurance that they must be restored to their own land, because it was from them that the Messiah was to proceed, and from them that the true religion was to be spread around the world'.[1]

The coming of Christ was, then, a comfort to those Jews who were captive in Babylon. We certainly do not share their circumstances, but we do often find ourselves disheartened and dispirited. There is comfort for us in Christ just as there was comfort for those captive Jews.

In fact, Isaiah's prophecy of Christ enables us to identify three major comforting truths about him.

He came to do a very comforting work

The Lord Jesus was assigned this work by the Father. Jesus was God's 'Elect One' (v. 1); that is, the one God chose to do the work. God not only chose him but also delights in him (v. 1).

Here is a spiritual principle to keep in mind — if we want God to delight in us, we must delight ourselves in what delights him. If God is delighted with Christ, we bring God's blessing into our own lives by delighting in Christ.

What was this work for which God chose the Lord Jesus Christ? This passage tells us some exhilarating things about the work of Christ.

It was a work on behalf of very needy, desperate people

God tells us that the Messiah would come to open the eyes of the blind (v. 7) and to release those in prison (v. 7).

What telling pictures these are for those who are apart from God! They are blind spiritually. They cannot see that God is holy. They cannot see their sinful condition. They cannot see the judgement that is rushing towards them. They cannot see the salvation provided by God. But Jesus Christ came to open blind eyes. On the basis of his finished work, the Holy Spirit has come to cause blind sinners to see the reality of these truths.

The Bible also teaches that we are all by nature imprisoned by Satan. He, like a strong man armed (Luke 11:21-22), stands guard over us. But Jesus Christ came to set sinners free. He himself said, 'Therefore if the Son makes you free, you shall be free indeed' (John 8:36).

It was a work of righteousness

Isaiah records these words spoken by God to the Messiah: 'I, the LORD, have called you in righteousness...' (v. 6). This might be rendered 'for a righteous purpose'. Albert Barnes says of Christ's work of salvation: 'In this work all was righteousness. God was righteous, who appointed him; it was because he was righteous, and could not save without a mediator and an atonement, that he sent him into the world; he selected one who was eminently righteous to accomplish his purpose; and he came that he might establish righteousness on the earth, and confirm the just government of God...'[2]

It was a work of justice

The Lord says the work of the Messiah would bring justice to the Gentiles (v. 1) and would establish it upon the earth (v. 4). Because God is holy, he cannot ignore or disregard our sins. He must judge them or cease to be holy. The Lord Jesus Christ could not release us from sins until the justice of God was satisfied against those sins. Christ satisfied that justice by going to Calvary's cross. There he received in his own person the wrath of God against his people so there is now no wrath left for them to endure.

It was a work of covenant (v. 6)

This means that it was a work by which God would make a covenant with sinners that he would be their God and they would be his people (2 Cor. 6:16, 18).

He has special tenderness for his feeble people

Tender gentleness would be one of the hallmarks of Jesus' life and ministry. This gentleness is set forth in two statements. First, the Lord God says of the coming Messiah:

> 'He will not cry out, nor raise his voice,
> Nor cause his voice to be heard in the street'
>
> (v. 2).

Derek Thomas writes: 'Have you ever listened to a sergeant major drilling his men? Jesus never dealt with his disciples that way. There was no screaming or shouting of orders. He did not assume the role of a military commander.'[3]

Secondly, the Lord says of the Messiah:

'A bruised reed he will not break,
And smoking flax he will not quench'

(v. 3).

The reed was a slender shoot from a plant. Shepherds would often fashion a small musical instrument from these reeds. But once such a reed was cracked it was useless for making music. The smoking flax is a reference to a candle that has almost gone out. All that remains is just a tiny, glowing ember on the wick.

God's people often feel like cracked reeds and smoking wicks. We often feel that we are both incapable of making music for the Lord and of reflecting light for him. There is good news for all who feel this way. The Lord does not break cracked reeds or quench smoking flax. He is sympathetic and understanding with our weaknesses. He does not cast us aside but offers restoration and renewal. In fact, far from breaking bruised reeds and quenching smoking wicks, the Lord Jesus actually restores them.

Down in the human heart,
Crushed by the tempter,
Feelings lie buried that grace can restore.
Touched by a loving heart,
Wakened by kindness,
Chords that are broken will vibrate once more.

Fanny Crosby, 'Rescue the Perishing'

We need only think of Simon Peter to find proof of this. He was very much a bruised reed and a smoking wick after denying the Lord Jesus three times. He undoubtedly thought the Lord would want nothing more to do with him. But the Lord Jesus tenderly took that bruised, smoking disciple and restored him to usefulness (John 21).

He himself will not fail in doing his work

The Lord God says of the Messiah:

'He will not fail nor be discouraged,
Till he has established justice in the earth...'

(v. 4).

This means the Messiah would not allow any opposition or hardship to throw him off course. He would persevere in the work the Father assigned him until it was done.

How much opposition the Lord Jesus encountered in his work! He was opposed at every point by Satan and hated by evil men. But he refused to deviate from the path the Father assigned him.

What is this work? It is the establishment of justice in the earth. By his work of redemption the Lord Jesus establishes a love for God's law in the hearts of his people, a love that makes them just and right in their conduct.

This work continues today and will continue until the Lord ushers his people into a new heaven and a new earth where they will love justice perfectly, and where righteousness will dwell (Rev. 21:1-4). All evil and evildoers will be banished from that glorious place, and justice will reign supreme (Rev. 21:8, 27).

The Lord will definitely have a people. Let there be no doubt about that. With the phrase 'the coastlands shall wait for his law' (v. 4), the Lord was promising that the gospel would reach even to the Gentiles and reap a great harvest of souls among them. Matthew Henry explains this promise by saying the Gentiles would bid the gospel welcome 'as if it had been a thing they had long waited for'. He further writes of the Gentiles: 'They shall become his disciples, shall sit at his feet, and be ready to receive the law from his mouth.'[4]

While the work of establishing justice in the earth is the Lord's, we who know him can participate in it. What a blessed privilege! Of course, we are not able to establish justice in human hearts, but we are able to proclaim the gospel which can; and, looking to the perseverance of our Lord, we can find encouragement to persevere in this proclamation.

Let the burdens and difficulties of life mount up around us! We have all the comfort we need in Christ. He came to do a comforting work. He did it with tender concern for his feeble people. And he himself was never feeble in doing this work of salvation.

What a Christ we have! Such a Christ is worthy of our joyful and faithful obedience and service.

For your journal...

1. List the ways in which you are comforted by the saving work of the Lord Jesus Christ.

2. Look through one of the four Gospels. Write down instances where Jesus treated bruised people in tender fashion.

3. Can you think of a time when you felt as if you were a bruised reed or a barely-flickering candle? Write down ways in which God tenderly dealt with you at that time.

Isaiah 43:1-7

But now, thus says the LORD, who created you, O Jacob,
And he who formed you, O Israel:
'Fear not, for as I have redeemed you;
I have called you by your name;
You are mine.
When you pass through the waters, I will be with you;
And through the rivers, they shall not overflow you.
When you walk through the fire, you shall not be burned,
Nor shall the flame scorch you.
For I am the LORD your God,
The Holy One of Israel, your Saviour;
I gave Egypt for your ransom,
Ethiopia and Seba in your place.
Since you were precious in my sight,
You have been honoured,
And I have loved you;
Therefore I will give men for you,
And people for your life.
Fear not, for I am with you;
I will bring your descendants from the east,
And gather you from the west;
I will say to the north, "Give them up!"
And to the south, "Do not keep them back!"

Bring my sons from afar,
And my daughters from the ends of the earth —
Everyone who is called by my name,
Whom I have created for my glory;
I have formed him, yes, I have made him.'

Day 4
The flood and the furnace

♦ *Begin by reading Isaiah 43*
♦ *Pray about what you have read*
♦ *Make notes on what you think God is teaching you*
♦ *Read the following chapter*
♦ *Answer the questions in the section 'For your journal'*

Isaiah 43:1-7

The prophet Isaiah lifted up his eyes to look at the future of his people and saw them going into a prolonged period of captivity in Babylon. As he contemplated this, he chose two emblems to convey something of what that experience would be like for his people: a flood of water and a furnace of fire.

These emblems must have seemed very fitting to those captives. The flood overwhelms and the fire consumes. Their circumstances were such that they often felt they simply could not cope any longer, as if they had come to the end of their resources. They must also have feared that they were about to be completely destroyed, that they as individuals and the nation as a whole would not survive.

The Lord gave Isaiah a cheering word for these beleaguered people. The water would not overwhelm them, and the fire would not consume them.

A twofold application

To the church

The primary application of this passage is, of course, to the church. She is the modern-day successor to the Israel of the Old Testament. And what a precious application this is! The church has often been in deep water and in flames of fire. It is no exaggeration to say that she is even now. The waters of scepticism and secularism mount up all about her, and the flames of affliction and persecution dance all around her.

But the church need not fear. She will not be overwhelmed, nor consumed. The world has often planned the church's funeral only to find there was no corpse in the casket.

The church will not fail because she belongs to the sovereign God. He placed his love upon her in eternity past and sent his Son to purchase her for himself. He loves the church, and has committed himself and all the resources of heaven to not only sustaining her in this world but also finally to bringing her safely into the presence of his glory. The Lord Jesus himself made clear the complete security of the church when he said of her: '…on this rock I will build my church, and the gates of Hades shall not prevail against it' (Matt. 16:18).

Let the devil and all his minions release from hell a mighty tide of destruction. There is no tide strong enough to drown the church. Let them stoke the furnace of affliction hotter than it has ever been before. There is no flame hot enough to consume the church. When human history is over and the sceptics and their theories have all passed away, the church they so hated will be enshrined in glory in Immanuel's land where she will shine with indescribable brilliance.

My word to all is this: Do not spend one moment of your time worrying about the final outcome for the church. Just make sure you are part of her through the redeeming work of Jesus Christ!

To individual believers

While the primary application of this passage must be as I have indicated, it is not the only application. It is also legitimate to extend the application to individual saints.

Suffering is an inevitable part of the Christian life. Please notice that the prophet, as he contemplated his nation's future, did not say, 'If you pass through the waters…' There was no uncertainty about it. He says, 'When you pass through the waters…' (v. 2).

The inevitability of suffering is taught consistently in Scripture. It is not the obscure teaching of one isolated passage in a little-known section of God's Word. The apostle Paul put it like this: 'Yes, and all who desire to live godly in Christ Jesus will suffer persecution' (2 Tim. 3:12). Paul and Barnabas assured the converts in Lystra, Iconium and Antioch that they must 'through many tribulations enter the kingdom of God' (Acts 14:22). The Lord Jesus himself made the certainty of suffering clear: 'Remember the word that I said to you, "A servant is not greater than his master." If they persecuted me, they will also persecute you' (John 15:20). On the basis of such verses, Alan Redpath says, 'God has had one Son without sin, but He has never had one child without suffering, never.'[1]

Are you, child of God, in the midst of suffering right now? Does it seem that the tide of persecution has so mounted up around you that it is going to sweep you away? Does the fire of affliction seem to be such a raging inferno that you feel it is going to consume you?

All kinds of difficult circumstances make us feel this way. It may be serious illness. It may be the serious illness or death of a loved one. It may be the crushing load of responsibility. It may be a fractured, tense relationship. It may be financial hardship. It may be a child that seems intent on breaking your heart and ruining both your life and his. What are we to do when our circumstances become like flood and fire?

There is consolation and solace for us in Isaiah's word to the captives of old. They are cheering words from the God of heaven. Ponder them well.

A cheering promise

There is a basic and fundamental promise here, stated twice. The Lord says, 'When you pass through the waters, I will be with you…' (v. 2). Later on, he adds: 'Fear not, for I am with you…' (v. 5).

> *How firm a foundation, ye saints of the Lord,*
> *Is laid for your faith in His excellent Word!*
> *What more can He say than to you He hath said,*
> *To you who for refuge to Jesus have fled?*
>
> *'Fear not, I am with thee; O be not dismayed,*
> *For I am thy God, and will still give thee aid;*
> *I'll strengthen thee, help thee, and cause thee to stand,*
> *Upheld by my righteous, omnipotent hand.*

'When through fiery trials thy pathway shall lie,
My grace all-sufficient shall be thy supply:
The flame shall not hurt thee; I only design
Thy dross to consume, and thy gold to refine.

'The soul that on Jesus hath leaned for repose
I will not, I will not desert to his foes;
That soul, though all hell should endeavour to shake,
I'll never, no, never, no, never forsake!'
                    George Keith, 'How Firm a Foundation'

The Lord's promise of his presence has often been used by
God's people to comfort each other. When another Christian
is facing difficulty and hardship, we almost instinctively ask
the Lord to be 'with' them, and we might even say to them:
'The Lord is with you.'

Have you ever wondered how this helps? How is the Lord
with his people in their trials and tribulations? What is there
about his presence that brings comfort to them? We can answer such questions by saying the Lord is with us in various
ways. He is with us as a *sympathizer*. He understands and cares.
He is with us as a *sustainer*. He is actually there to give us
strength, grace and wisdom, even when it seems that we are
completely without these things. He is with us as a wise
strategist. Everything he allows to come our way is for our
good and for his glory (Rom. 8:28). He is with us as a *preserver*.
Nothing, absolutely nothing, can ever destroy our relationship
with him. We are more than conquerors through him (8:37).
He is with as a *deliverer*. In his own time and way, he will
bring us through our difficulties. And, of course, the greatest
deliverance of all is when he finally takes us home to himself.
There nothing harmful or hurtful will ever be able to touch us
again.

The apostle Paul affirmed practically all these aspects of God's presence in these words: 'But the Lord stood with me and strengthened me ... Also I was delivered out of the mouth of the lion. And the Lord will deliver me from every evil work and preserve me for his heavenly kingdom. To him be glory for ever and ever. Amen!' (2 Tim. 4:17-18).

An unshakeable proof

All of this raises a very important and vital question, namely, how do we know the Lord is with us in these ways? That question is abundantly answered by the Lord in several phrases:

- 'the LORD ... created you ... and ... formed you' (v. 1)
- 'Fear not, for I have redeemed you' (v. 1)
- 'I have called you by your name' (v. 1)
- 'You are mine' (v. 1)
- 'I am the LORD your God' (v. 3)
- 'I gave Egypt for your ransom' (v. 3)
- 'You were precious in my sight' (v. 4)
- 'I have loved you' (v. 4)

This is the answer of redeeming love. The Lord would never allow his people to be completely overwhelmed and destroyed by their circumstances because they were his people. He loved them with an everlasting love. He had called them out of sin unto himself to be his own special possession. He had formed them as a people. He had even given up Egypt and other nations to destruction that he might save those he loved.

Redeeming love is the great theme of Scripture, and it is a strong and impregnable fortress for the children of God in every situation. Child of God, no matter what you are facing, run with it to the cross of Christ. There you will find comfort and strength.

The cross of Christ proves for ever how God feels about his people. Look long and hard at it. See the blood streaming down. See that disfigured face. Hear the voices of mockery, ridicule and scorn. See the sun hiding her face and darkness gathering all around. Hear that piercing cry: 'My God, my God, why have you forsaken me?', and understand as you hear it that Jesus Christ was there bearing your sin and the wrath it deserved.

Look long enough at Calvary's cross until this divine logic is drilled for ever into your heart — if God was willing to go to that extent to make us his children, we need never question that he will be with us in the flood and in the furnace.

For your journal...

1. Are the flood and furnace fitting emblems for trials that you have experienced? What trials have you found particularly distressing?

2. Write down ways in which you are helped by the knowledge of God's presence with you.

Isaiah 44:21-28

'Remember these, O Jacob,
And Israel, for you are my servant;
I have formed you, you are my servant;
O Israel, you will not be forgotten by me!
I have blotted out, like a thick cloud, your transgressions,
And like a cloud, your sins.
Return to me, for I have redeemed you.'

Sing, O heavens, for the LORD has done it!
Shout, you lower parts of the earth;
Break forth into singing, you mountains,
O forest, and every tree in it!
For the LORD has redeemed Jacob,
And glorified himself in Israel.

Thus says the LORD, your Redeemer,
And he who formed you from the womb:
'I am the LORD, who makes all things,
Who stretches out the heavens all alone,
Who spreads abroad the earth by myself;
Who frustrates the signs of the babblers,
And drives diviners mad;
Who turns wise men backward,
And makes their knowledge foolishness;

Who confirms the word of his servant,
And performs the counsel of his messengers;
Who says to Jerusalem, "You shall be inhabited,"
To the cities of Judah, "You shall be built,"
And I will raise up her waste places;
Who says to the deep, "Be dry!
And I will dry up your rivers";
Who says of Cyrus, "He is my shepherd,
And he shall perform all my pleasure,
Saying to Jerusalem, 'You shall be built,'
And to the temple, 'Your foundation shall be laid.'"'

Day 5
The devotions of God

- *Begin by reading Isaiah 44*
- *Pray about what you have read*
- *Make notes on what you think God is teaching you*
- *Read the following chapter*
- *Answer the questions in the section 'For your journal'*

Isaiah 44:21-28

To be devoted is to show strong affection or zeal for some-thing or someone. We are all devoted to something. Some are devoted to high and noble causes. Others are devoted to low and trivial things. Some are devoted only to themselves.

Have you ever thought about God being devoted to some-thing or someone? The Bible assures us that he is. In fact, this portion of Isaiah's prophecy displays two objects of God's fervent and faithful devotion.

God is devoted to his people (vv. 21-23)

It would not seem so. This part of Isaiah's prophecy was written for the people of God in captivity in Babylon. That circumstance made it appear that God had decisively rejected them, but these verses show that this was not the case.

The captivity was not proof of God's disregard for his people. It was just the opposite. It came about because God was so utterly devoted to them. It was his way of causing them to see their lack of devotion to him so that they might repent of it and return to him.

The verses before us contain three mighty affirmations of God's unfailing love for his people.

God's formation of his people

The Lord first says, 'I have formed you, you are my servant' (v. 21). God had made the people of Israel his own, so that they might serve him. God is not like us. We make plans, we try to accomplish them, we run into difficulties, we throw up our hands in despair and abandon our plans. But God does not abandon his. He faithfully executes each one, even to the point that Scripture says of him, 'Your counsels of old are faithfulness and truth' (Isa. 25:1).

God was not, therefore, about to give up on his plan for his people to serve him. But how does this prove God's devotion to his people? Because service carries a negative connotation, we might be inclined to regard this as proof that God held his people in very low esteem. If God really loved his people, he surely would not make them servants! So goes modern thinking!

But such a view fails to see that service to God is the highest privilege any mortal can enjoy. God does not make us servants because he desires to be mean to us or because he needs our service. He does so to ennoble and bless our lives. Making his people his servants is, then, a wonderful proof of his devotion to his people.

God's pledge to remember

Here is a second proof, that is, God's statement: 'O Israel, you will not be forgotten by me!' (v. 21). This is an explicit affirmation of God's love for his people. The Lord would later enlarge this affirmation with these compelling and powerful words:

'Can a woman forget her nursing child,
And not have compassion on the son of her womb?
Surely they may forget,
Yet I will not forget you.
See, I have inscribed you on the palms of my hands;
Your walls are continually before me'

(49:15-16).

These words leave no doubt about the matter. God was devoted to his people, so much so that their names were written indelibly on the palm of his hand, where they could always be seen; and the walls of their city, while lying in ruins, were still standing, as far as he was concerned.

God's forgiveness

That brings us to God's third statement of devotion: 'I have blotted out, like a thick cloud, your transgressions, and like a cloud, your sins' (v. 22). There can be no firmer proof of God's devotion than this — his forgiveness of their sins.

Sin is a very serious thing. Its seriousness is evident in the words God used to describe their failings. The word 'sin' itself means 'missing the mark' that God has set. The word 'transgression' means 'rebellion'. The people of Israel had been abundantly guilty of both.

Its seriousness is also evident in the figures God used for their sins. The phrase 'blotted out' suggests that sin leaves a permanent record. The reference to a cloud suggests that sin comes in a darkening and depressing way between the soul and God as a cloud blocks the rays of the sun.

What a terrible thing sin is! But what a wonderful thing forgiveness is! We cannot erase the handwriting of sin, but God can. We cannot remove the cloud of sin, but God can.

Part of the wonder of God's forgiveness is that he graciously supplies what he himself requires. He grants forgiveness to those who return to him, and he enables them to return! He does not say, 'Return and I will redeem.' He says, 'Return to me, for I have redeemed you' (v. 22).

God's free gift of forgiveness to guilty sinners has always been and continues to be on the basis of the redeeming work of his Son, Jesus Christ. God does not forgive sin by pretending it does not matter. That would compromise his justice. He is able to forgive sinners because Jesus paid for their sins. The Old Testament saints looked forward in faith to Jesus making that payment, while we look backward in faith to it.

No one who looks closely at Calvary's cross and the sin payment that God made there for his people can ever doubt that God loves his people. Those who have studied Calvary's love understand these words from Paul: 'He who did not spare his own Son, but delivered him up for us all, how shall he not with him also freely give us all things?' (Rom. 8:32).

It will take eternity itself to finally make plain God's tremendous devotion to his people. When eternity comes and reveals the extent of that devotion, those who have received it will stand amazed that God could ever have loved them in such a way, and they will most certainly be 'lost in wonder, love and praise'.

God is devoted to his Word (vv. 24-28)

We can divide this matter into two parts. First, God is affirming his zeal for his Word (vv. 25-26). Then God applies this to Israel's situation (vv. 26-28).

His affirmation

The Lord's affirmation itself consists of two parts. First, he speaks of his frustration of other words (v. 25). Secondly, he speaks of his confirmation of his own Word (v. 26). These words would have carried great meaning for the captives in Babylon. Before they went into captivity, they heard the messages of many prophets who told them that they were safe and secure. They also heard from prophets of the Lord who told them that captivity was imminent.

When the captivity came, the message of peace and security was proved to be false and the message of judgement was shown to be true. God had frustrated the false prophets and confirmed his own.

This has significance for us as well. Our own day features conflicting messages. On one hand, there is an abundance of voices that tell us we need not worry about what the Bible has to say about sin and judgement, that all will be well with us even if we disregard the Bible. On the other hand, we have the message of the Bible purporting to be the very Word of God.

We would do well to believe the latter message. Time after time it has been challenged and disputed only to prove true. The captives themselves could give testimony to this. They had embraced the message of the false prophets and spurned the message of God's prophets, and now they were in captivity. The Word of God had caught up with them (Zech. 1:4-6).

What is a Christian? He can be described from many angles, but … we can cover everything by saying: he is a man who acknowledges and lives under the word of God. He submits without reserve to the word of God written in 'the Scripture of truth' (Dan. 10:21), believing the teaching, trusting the promises, following the commands. His eyes are to the God of the Bible as his Father, and to Christ of the Bible as his Saviour. He will tell you, if you ask him, that the word of God has both convinced him of sin and assured him of forgiveness. His conscience, like Luther's, is captive to the word of God, and he aspires, like the psalmist, to have his whole life brought into line with it. 'O that my ways were directed to keep thy statutes!' 'O let me not wander from thy commandments.' 'Teach me thy statutes. Make me to understand the way of thy precepts.' 'Incline my heart unto thy testimonies.' 'Let my heart be sound in thy statutes' (Ps. 119:5, 10, 26f., 36, 80).

J. I. Packer, Knowing God[1]

His application

Let us turn now to consider the Lord's application. We know the captives in Babylon often wondered if there was any hope. Would their nation be restored or was she hopelessly and irretrievably lost? Would Jerusalem ever exist again? Would there ever be another temple? God addressed these concerns by emphatically saying to Jerusalem, 'You shall be built' and to the temple, 'Your foundation shall be laid' (v. 28).

As the captives pondered these words, it must have hit them like a sledgehammer that the same Word that had worked against them in the past was now working for them. In other words, the same Word that guaranteed their painful judgement in the past was now assuring them of a glorious future. If the former had proved to be true, there was no reason to doubt the latter.

We have here, then, a passage which vigorously affirms God's devoted zeal for both his people and his Word. Now here is a point of application for us to ponder thoroughly. If God so delights in his people and his Word, what should we do if we want to please him and obtain his blessing? Isn't the answer obvious? We should delight in his people and his Word! And as God's delight in these things is evident from the things he did, our delight in these same things will manifest itself in how we live.

For your journal...

1. If God is devoted to his people, does it not follow that even our trials and afflictions are evidences of his devotion? Write down ways in which trials are for the good of God's people.

2. Make a list of others who are going through serious trials. Remember to pray for them. What can you do to help them?

Isaiah 45:22-25

'Look to me, and be saved,
All you ends of the earth!
For I am God, and there is no other.
I have sworn by myself;
The word has gone out of my mouth in righteousness,
And shall not return,
That to me every knee shall bow,
Every tongue shall take an oath.
He shall say,
"Surely in the Lord I have righteousness and strength.
To him men shall come,
And all shall be ashamed
Who are incensed against him.
In the Lord all the descendants of Israel
Shall be justified, and shall glory."'

Day 6
A gracious invitation and a solemn warning

- ♦ *Begin by reading Isaiah 45*
- ♦ *Pray about what you have read*
- ♦ *Make notes on what you think God is teaching you*
- ♦ *Read the following chapter*
- ♦ *Answer the questions in the section 'For your journal'*

Isaiah 45:22-25

Our text begins with these words from the Lord:

'Look to me, and be saved,
All you ends of the earth!
For I am God, and there is no other.'

These are some of the best-known and most-loved words in all the Bible. They offer the single greatest blessing that God has to bestow, that is, the blessing of salvation from sin. How often guilty, aching sinners have found that salvation by hearing the cheering words of this verse!

On Sunday morning, 6 January 1850, a young man was making his way to church. A very heavy snowfall and bitter cold caused him to stop short of his intended destination and to enter the Artillery Street Primitive Methodist Chapel in Colchester, Essex. The announced preacher, apparently hindered by the same storm, did not arrive. After waiting for a few minutes, one of the deacons went to the pulpit. He took the words of Isaiah 45:22 as his text and delivered a very simple sermon. At one point he looked at the young man, and said, 'Young man, you look very miserable, and you will be miserable, miserable in life and in death if you don't obey my text. But if you obey now, you will be saved. Young man, look to Jesus Christ! Look! Look! Look! You have nothin' to do but to look and live.'

Charles Spurgeon was converted then and there and went on to conduct one of the most powerful gospel ministries in history.

This wonderful text comes at the close of a long section in which the Lord God assures his people that their captivity in Babylon would have a happy end, namely, their deliverance. Yet the Lord could not be content to speak only of that deliverance. He used that political deliverance to speak of a different kind of deliverance, and one that was far greater: deliverance from sin.

The invitation offered

The benefit offered

There are three things for us to notice about this invitation. First, there is the benefit that is offered. It is right there in that word 'saved'. We understand this word. To be saved means that we have been rescued from a terrible threat or danger. What is the danger from which God offers to rescue us? It is the danger posed by our sinful condition. Because of our sin we stand under the condemnation of God. That means that we are not only separated from God in this life, but will also be separated from him in the life to come in a condition the Bible calls 'everlasting destruction' (2 Thess. 1:9).

What a solemn and terrifying thought! What reasonable person would not want to be delivered from such a calamity! But how can one have such deliverance? This passage gives us the answer.

The means by which the benefit is secured

The Lord puts it in these words: 'Look to me...' With these simple words, he essentially says, 'If you want salvation from your sins, you must look to me. I am the one who provides it.'

How has the Lord provided salvation? Through his Son, Jesus Christ! It is true that there is no mention of Christ in the passage before us, but the word 'saved' is here and Scripture often connects that word with Christ (Matt. 1:21; Luke 19:10; John 3:17; 5:34; 12:47). Furthermore, the prophecy of Isaiah itself will soon explicitly connect salvation from sin with the Lord Jesus Christ (53:4-11).

The Lord Jesus came to this earth to be the means of salvation for sinners. He came to live the righteous life that they could not live and to die the death they deserved to die. Through him sinners can have the righteousness that God demands and secure payment for their sins.

Salvation is in Christ Jesus. But how do we receive it? We must 'look' to him! There is no need to complicate that word.

To look means to trust. If I tell you that I look to a plumber to handle my plumbing problems, you know immediately what I am saying. I am relying or depending completely upon the plumber to solve the problems.

> *The word is 'look', not 'labour' or 'serve'. These things are the results of salvation, but salvation and eternal life are the gift of God through the person and work of Christ. Only believe and live!*
>
> *Henry T. Mahan,* With New Testament Eyes[1]

If you want the salvation provided by God in his Son, you must completely rely or depend upon Christ. You must pin all your hopes on him. This means you must look away from everything else. You cannot be saved if you look to good works. You cannot be saved if you look to church membership. You cannot be saved if you look to anything or anyone other than the Lord Jesus.

The Lord makes this abundantly clear right here in our passage. He says, 'I am God, and there is no other' (v. 22). There is no other God, and there is, therefore, no other way to be saved except the way that he himself has designed and ordained.

We need now to notice a final point about this invitation.

The ones to whom this benefit is offered

There is no difficulty here. The invitation is addressed to the 'ends of the earth' (v. 22). It is addressed to all. And there is, of course, a very sound reason for this. All need to be saved. We all come into this world in the sinful condition that leads finally to eternal separation. Since we are all in that condition, we all need salvation.

How thankful we should be that there is such a wideness in God's mercy! It is so wide that he will turn no one away. Revelation 22:17 trumpets this truth in these cheering words: 'And the Spirit and the bride say, "Come!" And let him who hears say, "Come!" And let him who thirsts come. Whoever desires, let him take the water of life freely.'

The solemn warning

The Lord says:

> '…I am God, and there is no other.
> I have sworn by myself;
> The word has gone out of my mouth in righteousness,
> And shall not return,
> That to me every knee shall bow,
> Every tongue shall take an oath'
>
> (vv. 22-23).

The option facing each and every one of us is quite simple. We either bow before God in this life and acknowledge that he is truly God or we bow before him in the life to come. But we will all bow! God has sworn it, and every single one of us will do it.

These two possibilities are not equal. If we bow before God now and accept his invitation, we receive his salvation. If we refuse to bow now, our bowing later will not save us. We will bow before God to acknowledge the truth about him before we are driven from his presence into eternal woe. It is of crucial importance, then, to bow before him now.

What a happy testimony we have in these verses from the one who bows before the Lord in this life!

'Surely in the Lord I have righteousness and strength...
In the Lord all the descendants of Israel
Shall be justified and shall glory'

(vv. 24-25).

Yes, this is the testimony of the one who accepts God's invitation to salvation. This person realizes that he has all he needs in the Lord. And he realizes that 'all the descendants of Israel', that is, all believers in the Lord have a right standing before God and eternal glory awaiting them. The believer is happy indeed!

But as he testifies to his happiness in the Lord, he cannot help but take note of those who refuse God's invitation. Of them he says:

'And all shall be ashamed
Who are incensed against him'

(v. 24).

Can words be clearer? All those who reject God's invitation will finally come to shame. Perhaps someone will deny that these words apply to him. He may argue that it is possible to reject God's invitation and not be incensed against God. But God does not look at it that way. He says we are either for him or against him (Matt. 12:30). There is no middle ground.

If we are against him and remain against him throughout this life, we will come to shame in the life to come. No shame with which we are familiar can compare with that shame — the shame of standing in the presence of almighty God with the realization that he graciously gave us the opportunity to be saved and we spurned it.

If you want to avoid that incredible shame, you must here and now heed God's warning and accept his invitation. Yes, I say to you the same thing that deacon said to young Charles Spurgeon: 'Look to Jesus and live.'

For your journal...

1. Do you feel deep gratitude for God's gracious invitation? Write a prayer of thanksgiving and praise to God for his salvation.

2. Read Matthew 22:1-14 for an example of one who rejected God's gracious invitation. Does this account make you think of family members and friends who are doing the same? Make a list of these and begin praying daily for them.

Isaiah 46:3-4, 9-10, 12-13

'Listen to me, O house of Jacob,
And all the remnant of the house of Israel,
Who have been upheld by me from birth,
Who have been carried from the womb:
Even to your old age, I am he,
And even to grey hairs, I will carry you!
I have made, and I will bear;
Even I will carry, and will deliver you.

…

'Remember the former things of old,
For I am God, and there is no other;
I am God, and there is none like me,
Declaring the end from the beginning,
And from ancient times things that are not yet done,
Saying, "My counsel shall stand,
And I will do all my pleasure."

…

'Listen to me, you stubborn-hearted,
Who are far from righteousness:
I bring my righteousness near, it shall not be far off;
My salvation shall not linger.
And I will place salvation in Zion,
For Israel my glory.'

Day 7
Three unfailing things

♦ *Begin by reading Isaiah 46*
♦ *Pray about what you have read*
♦ *Make notes on what you think God is teaching you*
♦ *Read the following chapter*
♦ *Answer the questions in the section 'For your journal'*

Isaiah 46:3-4, 9-10, 12-13

One of the saddest parts of life is that things fail. Friendships fail. Families fail. Finances fail. Health fails.

The poor captives in Babylon must often have thought that every part of their lives had failed, that there was absolutely nothing they could count on or depend on. Their kings had failed them. Their military had failed them. Many of their religious leaders had failed them. And now in Babylon they must have found themselves wondering what they had left.

All they had to do to find the answer to that probing question was to read this portion of Isaiah's prophecy, the prophecy they had carried with them into captivity. Here the Lord triumphantly and emphatically tells them that he had not failed them and would not fail them. Indeed, he reminds them of

three truths to confirm this. Lest they let any of these truths
slip past them, he attaches to each one a passionate appeal to
his people to pay heed. Twice he says, 'Listen to me' (vv. 3,
12), and once he says, 'Remember this' (v. 8).

These truths apply to us. And what cheering truths they
are! In days of uncertainty it is good to be able to identify
certain and unshakeable things. The failings in life should
make us appreciate more those things that cannot fail.

God's unfailing care for his people (vv. 1-7)

The Lord assured the captives in Babylon of this truth by saying
that he would continue to carry them (v. 4). He had carried
them from their birth as a nation, and he would continue to
carry them even though they were now advanced in years.
Such was his care for them!

Along with this marvellous assurance, the Lord gave them
a very sharp reminder of why they were in captivity. It was not
because he, the Lord, had failed them, but rather because they
had forsaken him to worship idols.

What a contrast he draws between himself and these idols!
While he had carried his people, they themselves had to carry
their idols. Those very idols, in which they had trusted, had
not been able to deliver them from their captivity. In fact,
their captors had carried their idols into captivity along with
the people (v. 2).

How desperately we need this word! This very day multitudes are doing what the people of Isaiah did so long ago.
They are giving to idols the worship and the devotion that
belongs to God alone. Some worship and serve money, some
pleasure, and some their career. All who do so would do well

to heed the stern warning of this passage — our idols have to be carried! When we make an idol of something, at first it may seem very wonderful and enjoyable, but it will eventually prove to be a heavy load. Those who are involved in various addictions can give powerful testimony to this.

And that is not all. Our idols will also prove to be of no help when the storms of life descend! But the true and living God is not a burden, but a burden-bearer. He is not a load to us but a lift for us. He does not have to be carried around; he carries us. He says to his people:

> Cast your burden on the LORD,
> And he shall sustain you...
>
> (Ps. 55:22).

The apostle Peter says we should cast our cares upon him because he cares for us (1 Peter 5:7). How can we be assured of this? How do we know the Lord is a burden-bearing God? All we have to do is look to the cross of Christ. There God answered once and for all the question of whether he cares for his people. He put his Son, Jesus Christ, on that cross precisely because he, God, is a burden-bearing God. There the Lord Jesus took the burden of our sins so we, his people, do not have to bear those sins and the punishment they deserve. In so doing, Jesus fulfilled these words from Isaiah:

> Surely he has borne our griefs
> And carried our sorrows
>
> (53:4).

Look to the cross, and you will never again doubt that God is a burden-bearing God.

Rest then, believer, upon the God who carries his people. Rejoice in knowing that he began carrying you when he made you his child, that he still carries you today, and that he will not stop until he carries you safely to heaven itself where he will set you down in glory that is unimaginable. E. J. Young observes: 'When man carries his god the end is destruction; when the true God carries man, the end is salvation.'[1]

God's unfailing purpose (vv. 8-11)

The Lord says:

'My counsel shall stand,
And I will do all my pleasure'

(v. 10).

That word 'counsel' means 'purpose', 'design' or 'will'. We are to understand then that God has a will or a purpose regarding human affairs. We are to further understand that nothing can ultimately frustrate or thwart that purpose.

> ... it is a matter of unspeakable joy that God **has** a plan, and that it will be executed... If there were **no plan** in relation to human things, the mind could find no rest. If there was no evidence that One Mind presided over human affairs; that an infinitely wise plan had been formed, and that all things had been adjusted so as best to secure the ultimate accomplishment of that plan, everything would have the appearance of chaos, and the mind must be filled with doubts and distractions. But our anxieties vanish in regard to the apparent irregularities and disorders of the universe, when we feel that all things are under

the direction of an Infinite Mind, and will be made to accom-
plish his plan, and further his great designs (emphasis his).
> *Albert Barnes,* Notes on the Old Testament: Isaiah[2]

In this passage God applies the firmness of his purpose to the deliverance of his people from Babylon. He would use a pagan king (previously identified as Cyrus: 44:28; 45:1) as his 'bird of prey' (46:11) to swoop down upon the Babylonians and set the captives free. Some might receive such an announcement with doubt and scepticism. What about this eventuality? What about such a possibility? Could not such things thwart God's plan and defeat his intention?

To all who were inclined to think this way, this passage affirms that God's plan was set and nothing could change or defeat it. With God there are no unforeseen circumstances. He declares 'the end from the beginning' (v. 10). That means he can start at the beginning and say accurately what is going to happen all the way through to the end.

With a sovereign God, there are no eventualities. There are only actualities. And what appears to us to be at odds with God's plan will finally prove to be part of it all along.

God's unfailing demand and provision for righteousness (vv. 12-13)

The Lord says:

> 'I bring my righteousness near, it shall not be far off;
> My salvation shall not linger.
> And I will place salvation in Zion,
> For Israel my glory.'

We should not be surprised that this chapter closes with these verses. The Lord has just promised deliverance from captivity for his people. That would be an act of unspeakable mercy and grace. But lest the people should think this act of mercy indicated that God treated sin lightly, he adds this word about his righteousness or justice.

How very hard it is for us to understand these matters! God loves sinners and forgives them their sins, but he never does so at the expense of his justice. His mercy is always extended with the approval and satisfaction of that justice.

Evangelical commentators have long regarded the closing verses of Isaiah 46 as nothing less than a prophecy of the coming Christ. It is quite impossible to encounter that word 'salvation' (v. 13) without thinking of Christ. He was sent to purchase eternal salvation for his people (Matt. 1:21), and the political and temporal deliverances of the people of God down through the centuries are only faint representations of that greatest of all deliverances — deliverance from sin through Christ.

But let us pay careful attention to how God went about providing eternal salvation through Christ. It was through perfectly blending mercy and justice and by satisfying both. When Jesus died on the cross, mercy was satisfied because Jesus made the way for sinners to be forgiven. But justice was also satisfied because Jesus bore on that cross the wrath of God against sinners. We might say mercy and justice came together at the cross and kissed each other.

Those who reject what God did on the cross to satisfy his justice will experience that justice in eternity.

For your journal...

1. What evidences of God's care in your life can you see? Write them down. Think about where you would be without them. Thank God for them.

2. Do you often struggle with anxiety and worry? Do you find help in knowing that God's purpose for you will not fail?

Isaiah 47:1-4

'Come down and sit in the dust,
O virgin daughter of Babylon;
Sit on the ground without a throne,
O daughter of the Chaldeans!
For you shall no more be called
Tender and delicate.
Take the millstones and grind meal.
Remove your veil,
Take off the skirt,
Uncover the thigh,
Pass through the rivers.
Your nakedness shall be uncovered,
Yes, your shame will be seen;
I will take vengeance,
And I will not arbitrate with a man.'

As for our Redeemer, the LORD of hosts is his name,
The Holy One of Israel.

Day 8
Double comfort

♦ *Begin by reading Isaiah 47*
♦ *Pray about what you have read*
♦ *Make notes on what you think God is teaching you*
♦ *Read the following chapter*
♦ *Answer the questions in the section 'For your journal'*

Isaiah 47:1-4

There are two speakers in the fifteen verses of this chapter. The Lord speaks in fourteen of them; the prophet Isaiah speaks in the other one (v. 4).

It might appear that the only comfort to be found in this chapter is in the one verse from the prophet. What the Lord has to say seems to be very dark and foreboding. There is, of course, comfort in what Isaiah had to say, but there is also comfort in what the Lord had to say. So, here is double comfort. In Isaiah's brief interjection, we find the comfort of God's grace. In the Lord's words, we find the comfort of God's justice.

Let us look first at the latter.

The comfort of God's justice

The Lord here speaks to Babylon about the judgement that he was going to send upon her. It was to be a crushing and devastating judgement. The chapter begins with the Lord saying:

> 'Come down and sit in the dust,
> O virgin daughter of Babylon;
> Sit on the ground without a throne,
> O daughter of the Chaldeans!'

The Lord addresses Babylon as 'virgin daughter' because she had never been conquered. All that would change. Babylon would collapse and she would sit in the dust.

Some would be inclined to attribute the fall of Babylon to the changing tides of political fortune, but the Lord makes it plain that her fall would come because of him. He says, 'I will take vengeance' (v. 3).

Why would the Lord treat Babylon so severely? Was it because he was cruel and heartless? No, it was because Babylon had been cruel and heartless. The Lord had allowed Babylon to take his people into captivity because his people had sinned against him and needed correction. But Babylon had 'showed them no mercy' (v. 6). She had also allowed herself to be filled with pride. She thought she was invincible (vv. 7-8, 10). Furthermore, she had trusted in sorcery and astrology (vv. 9, 12-15).

In sending his people into Babylon, the Lord, as the book of Daniel makes clear, had done that pagan nation a great favour. Through Daniel and others the Lord had brought the light of his truth to that land, so much so that the king of

Babylon, Nebuchadnezzar, actually said, 'Now I, Nebuchadnezzar, praise and extol and honour the King of heaven, all of whose works are truth, and his ways justice. And those who walk in pride he is able to put down' (Dan. 4:37).

But even with the Lord's truth shining brightly in Babylon, her leaders and her people refused to turn their backs on their idols and receive that truth. They continued to embrace their sorcery and their astrology.

They were about to learn how foolish they were. The Lord's judgement was going to fall upon them, and all their astrologers and prognosticators would be unable to prevent it (vv. 12-15).

The Lord, then, had good reasons for bringing judgement upon Babylon. But the question we have to ask is whether this chapter on judgement belongs in what we have been calling 'God's Book of Comfort', or have we been wrong to refer to this part of Isaiah in this way? To put it another way, can God's people find comfort in God's judgement?

Many do not hesitate to say a hearty 'No!' As far as they are concerned, God is loving and kind, and judgement is out of keeping with his loving nature. They find it necessary, therefore, to find an alternative meaning for passages such as Isaiah 47. They do so in various ways. Some say that such passages are wrong; that God is not really like that, but the men who wrote these passages about judgement mistakenly attributed to God something that is foreign to him. Others say that God indeed acted this way during the Old Testament era, but now he has changed to being kind and loving.

When we have difficulty accepting the teachings of Scripture on a given point, it is often very helpful to ask this question: What would we have if this teaching were not here? As we come to a passage that lays before us the reality of God's judgement, let us raise this question. In other words, what I am asking is whether we can be happy in saying that there is no moral authority in this universe. Are we happy to say that people can and should be able to carry out all the evil they want without fear of punishment? Can Adolf Hitler plunge a world into war, cause unspeakable suffering, run up a huge toll of innocent lives and God simply say, 'It's okay!' Do we want God to be like that? Do we want him to look upon Timothy McVeigh's wanton destruction of human life in Oklahoma City, USA, in April 1995, and say it is okay?

Do we really want the drug pushers, the pornographers and the child abusers to walk free? When we think along these lines most of us have our answer. Yes, there is comfort in God's justice! There is comfort in knowing that while evil men and women can escape justice in our human courts, they will eventually come into a court where they will receive what is right and fair.

We can indeed find comfort in God's justice. But, thank God that we can find comfort in this as well — there is more to God than justice. Now we will return to the first of our two points.

The comfort of God's grace

Verse 4, as we have noted, is an interjection from the prophet Isaiah. He is reporting what the Lord had to say about the forthcoming judgement of Babylon, and as he reports he is suddenly struck with the knowledge that he and all people of faith have something for which to be tremendously thankful.

Of verse 4, Barnes writes: 'This verse stands absolutely, and is not connected with the preceding or the following. It seems to be an expression of admiration, or of grateful surprise, by which the prophet saw JEHOVAH as the Redeemer of his people. He saw, in vision, Babylon humbled, and, full of the subject, he breaks out into an expression of grateful surprise and rejoicing.'

Albert Barnes, Notes on the Old Testament: Isaiah[1]

Isaiah recognized that he and his people were in a different category. The kind of judgement that God was determined to bring upon Babylon would never be experienced by the people of God.

Yes, the Lord does chastise his people when they sin against him. The presence of his people in Babylon gave powerful testimony to that (v. 6). But there is all the difference in the world between the temporary chastisement of God's people for their correction and the complete and final judgement of unbelievers to their destruction.

There was no doubt in Isaiah's mind about how he and his fellow-believers had come to escape the kind of judgement that would befall Babylon. It was all God's doing. God was their Redeemer. This God, who is sovereign over all the angelic hosts of heaven, had stooped in grace to redeem his people. 'The Holy One of Israel' had stooped to save guilty, undeserving sinners (v. 4).

Isaiah was utterly amazed at such grace. He was filled with worship and praise. While God was visiting others in judgement, he, Isaiah, and his people were redeemed. While the storm was breaking with fury on others, the people of God were sheltered and safe.

Those of us who know the Lord rejoice with Isaiah. We know the truth of what he says, because we ourselves have been delivered from God's eternal wrath. We acknowledge that our deliverance is not because of any good that resides in us; it is entirely due to the grace of God.

Now here is the marvel of God's saving grace: he does not bestow it at the expense of his justice. It is bestowed in and through the redeeming death of his Son, Jesus Christ. As we have noted, on the cross the Lord Jesus satisfied God's justice. He received the penalty that God's justice demands for our sins. Since Jesus received that penalty, there is nothing left for his people to pay. Because our penalty has been paid, we do not have to fear eternal separation from God, but we can look forward to sharing eternal glory with him.

While we wait for that glory, we live in Babylon. We live in a world in which God's truth is denigrated and false teachings abound. It is our great responsibility and our joyous privilege, while we live in Babylon, to do as Isaiah did, that is, to give testimony to the redeeming grace that has touched our lives. As we do so, we may rejoice in knowing that even the Babylonians among whom we live do not have to experience God's judgement but may also receive that grace.

For your journal...

1. How do you respond to the thought of comfort in God's justice?

2. How are you testifying to the redeeming grace of God? Write down any additional things you can do.

Isaiah 48:17-22

*Thus says the L*ORD*, your Redeemer,*
The Holy One of Israel:
*'I am the L*ORD *your God,*
Who teaches you to profit,
Who leads you by the way you should go.
Oh, that you had heeded my commandments!
Then your peace would have been like a river,
And your righteousness like the waves of the sea.
Your descendants also would have been like the sand,
And the offspring of your body like the grains of sand;
His name would not have been cut off
Nor destroyed from before me.'

Go forth from Babylon!
Flee from the Chaldeans!
With a voice of singing,
Declare, proclaim this,
Utter it to the end of the earth;
*Say, 'The L*ORD *has redeemed his servant Jacob!'*
And they did not thirst
When he led them through the deserts;
He caused the waters to flow from the rock for them;
He also split the rock, and the waters gushed out.

*'There is no peace,' says the L*ORD*, 'for the wicked.'*

Day 9
Setting the record straight

- *Begin by reading Isaiah 48*
- *Pray about what you have read*
- *Make notes on what you think God is teaching you*
- *Read the following chapter*
- *Answer the questions in the section 'For your journal'*

Isaiah 48:17-22

A lot of people are unhappy with God. They think he is trying to spoil their happiness, and that he is most happy when they are unhappy. They think he gave us certain commandments for the sole purpose of making life miserable. They believe he delights in bringing judgement upon people.

Much of the current fascination with angels is due to the fact that many people are unhappy with God. They view angels as being soft, cuddly and helpful, while they see God as mean and harsh. The Jews who were taken captive to Babylon may very well have harboured similar thoughts about God. They may have been inclined to explain their captivity in terms of God spoiling their happiness and rejoicing in their calamity.

In the verses before us God sets the record straight. He lets his people peek into his heart to see what he is really like. It is a glimpse that all of us need to share. Nothing is more important for our personal happiness and well-being than gaining an accurate understanding of what God is truly like.

What do these verses entitle us to say about God and the afflictions he sends his people?

God's kind purpose in sending afflictions

First, we can say the Lord has a kind and benevolent purpose in the afflictions of his people (v. 17). Captivity in Babylon had to be a very taxing and unpleasant experience. But it did not prove that God was unkind to his people; it proved just the opposite. God brought this particular form of affliction upon his people so that they would 'profit' from it, so he could lead them the way they should go.

What was the way in which God wanted them to walk? It was the pathway of righteousness, the pathway of obedience to his commandments. This is the pathway to blessing and peace. The Lord says his people would have had peace 'like a river' and righteousness 'like the waves of the sea' (v. 18) if they had obeyed his commandments.

The word 'peace' refers to 'wholeness' or 'soundness'. It refers to good of every kind.[1] 'Righteousness' refers to holiness and purity. By using the emblems of the river and the waves of the sea, God was saying that he wanted his people to enjoy both peace and righteousness in abundance.

When someone suggests that God's way of living is the way of misery, that it spoils our fun and ruins our happiness, they are spreading the lie of the devil. Yes, there are difficulties in walking the Lord's way. There is definitely a yoke in Christianity. But it is the way of transgressors that is truly hard. The life of sin offers no real peace and no real joy. It may appear to do so, but in the end it will prove to bring only misery and woe (Isa. 48:22; 57:21). Compared to the hardship exacted by the life of sin, the yoke of Christianity is very easy and its burden very light (Matt. 11:28-30).

> *...though God's thoughts concerning the body of that people were thoughts of peace, yet to those among them that were wicked and hated to be reformed there is no peace, no peace with God or their own consciences, no real good, whatever is pretended to. What have those to do with peace who are enemies to God? Their false prophets cried Peace to those to whom it did not belong; but God tells them that there shall be no peace, nor anything like it, to the wicked. The quarrel sinners have commenced with God, if not taken up in time by repentance, will be an everlasting quarrel.*
>
> *Matthew Henry,* Matthew Henry's Commentary[2]

The people of God went into captivity in Babylon, then, because the Lord had their best interest at heart. They were there so they could learn the folly of disobeying God and the wisdom of obeying him. They were there for their own profit. They were there so their nation could, upon their return to their own land, enjoy the peace and righteousness that comes through obedience. They were there because the Lord was chastising them.

Chastisement is not something that God did in Old Testament times but has since abandoned. The author of Hebrews writes:

'My son, do not despise the
    chastening of the LORD,
Nor be discouraged when you
    are rebuked by him;
For whom the LORD loves he chastens,
And scourges every son whom he receives'

                                  (Heb. 12:5-6).

What is the Lord's purpose in doing this? It is 'for our profit, that we may be partakers of his holiness' (v. 10), so our lives will yield 'the peaceable fruit of righteousness' (v. 11).

Chastisement is not God getting even with his people for their sins. He did that on the cross. It is God helping them to be what they ought to be for their own well-being. God's chastisement is designed to bring us to the point where we are able to say to the Lord:

Before I was afflicted I went astray,
But now I keep your word ...
I know, O LORD, that your judgements are right,
And that in faithfulness you have afflicted me

                                (Psa. 119:67, 75).

God's grief in sending afflictions

Our text also compels us to draw a second conclusion about the Lord sending affliction on his people; that is, that he grieves when such afflictions are necessary. Here we find the Lord looking upon the captivity of his people in Babylon and crying: 'Oh, that you had heeded my commandments!' (v. 18).

God takes no pleasure in chastisement any more than a loving father takes pleasure in disciplining his children. We find the tender heart of God displayed in these words he spoke to Israel through Hosea the prophet:

'How can I give you up, Ephraim?
How can I hand you over, Israel?
How can I make you like Admah?
How can I set you like Zeboiim?
My heart churns within me;
My sympathy is stirred'

(11:8).

God grieves, then, over the chastisement of his people. But we can also say that he rejoices when his chastisement achieves its purpose, and his people come to see their sin, turn their backs upon it and return to him.

To see this truth we have to look no further than our Lord's parable of the prodigal son. The son had rebelled mightily against his father. He had asked his father for his inheritance, which was tantamount to saying that he wished his father were dead so he could have immediately what would be due to him then. He then went into the far country and wasted all the money his father gave him.

The father could surely have predicted what would happen. He knew his son would end up in poverty and ruin. And the father could have said something like this to himself: 'One day he will come crawling back to me, and when he does, I am going to say: "You made your choice. You wanted to leave home. Now you are going to have to accept the consequences."'

Things turned out just as the father knew they would. His son did indeed end up in poverty, and, yes, he came crawling home. But the father did not send him away. No, the father saw his son coming home, felt compassion for him, ran to him and 'fell on his neck and kissed him'. Then, turning to his servants, the father said, 'Bring out the best robe and put it on him, and put a ring on his hand and sandals on his feet. And bring the fatted calf here and kill it, and let us eat and be merry; for this my son was dead and is alive again; he was lost and is found' (Luke 15:22-24).

God's determination to redeem

A final truth for us to learn about the Lord and the afflictions of his people is that he will finally redeem his people from all their afflictions. This passage does not end with the Lord griev-ing over the affliction of his people. It ends with the Lord saying to them:

> Go forth from Babylon!
> Flee from the Chaldeans!
> With a voice of singing,
> Declare, proclaim this,
> Utter it to the end of the earth;
> Say, 'The LORD has redeemed
> His servant Jacob!'

(v. 20).

We must be clear on this. Not all the afflictions of God's people come upon them because the Lord is chastising them. Some-times the Lord puts his people into positions of hardship so they can there give testimony to the grace of the Lord and lead others to Christ. Most of the time afflictions come upon his people simply because they are part of this world, and this is what this world is like. The world has been scarred by sin, and no one walks through it without being scarred themselves.

But whatever the cause of the afflictions of God's people, this much we know for sure: their afflictions are limited to this life. The Lord will finally take his people to himself. He will give them a new heaven and a new earth and he 'will wipe away every tear from their eyes; there shall be no more death, nor sorrow, nor crying. There shall be no more pain, for the former things have passed away' (Rev. 21:4).

While we wait for that day, let us learn to say with the apostle Paul: 'And the Lord will deliver me from every evil work and preserve me for his heavenly kingdom. To him be glory for ever and ever. Amen!' (2 Tim. 4:18).

For your journal...

1. Have you been unhappy with God because of difficulties he has allowed to come into your life? Have you considered the possibility that these difficulties might be an expression of his tender concern for you? Write a prayer of thanksgiving to God for all things — even the difficulties!

2. Read carefully the account of the prodigal son (Luke 15:11-24). Write down the lessons that occur to you from this parable.

Isaiah 49:13-16

Sing, O heavens!
Be joyful, O earth!
And break out in singing, O mountains!
For the L<small>ORD</small> has comforted his people,
And will have mercy on his afflicted.

But Zion said, 'The L<small>ORD</small> has forsaken me,
And my Lord has forgotten me.'

'Can a woman forget her nursing child,
And not have compassion on the son of her womb?
Surely they may forget,
Yet I will not forget you.
See, I have inscribed you on the palms of my hands;
Your walls are continually before me.'

Day 10
For those who feel forgotten by God

- ◆ *Begin by reading Isaiah 49*
- ◆ *Pray about what you have read*
- ◆ *Make notes on what you think God is teaching you*
- ◆ *Read the following chapter*
- ◆ *Answer the questions in the section 'For your journal'*

Isaiah 49:13-16

There are three speakers in these verses. The prophet Isaiah speaks in verse 13, delivering God's message to the captives in Babylon. It is a message of assurance and comfort. He exhorts them to sing and be joyful, assuring them that the Lord would have mercy on them.

The nature of God's mercies is not hard to determine. For one thing, the Lord would deliver his people from captivity and restore them to their homeland. The Lord would also send the Messiah in due time. There was, then, great reason for rejoicing.

The second speaker in these verses is the captive (v. 14). All the captives join their individual voices to speak as one and to object to what Isaiah has just said to them. He has called them to sing and to rejoice, but they felt as if they had no reason to rejoice. Their circumstances were such that they felt the Lord had completely abandoned them.

It is at this point that these verses begin to speak so very pointedly and powerfully to us. Many of God's people find themselves in the very same situation as these captives of old. They find on one hand that they are commanded by Scripture to rejoice and be comforted, but on the other hand their circumstances are such that they feel that this is impossible for them. They are caught, as it were, between the command of their God and the difficulty of their situation. They see their circumstances to be such that God seems to have completely forsaken them. They feel abandoned by the very God who commands them to rejoice.

Does it seem to you this day that the Lord has forsaken you? Does it seem that he is very far away and cares nothing at all for you? There is certainly no shortage of circumstances to make us come to this conclusion. Serious illness can make us feel abandoned. The death of family members and friends can do the same. So can the loss of employment and the fracture of relationships.

How very timely are verses 13 and 14! They reflect a constant and ongoing reality in the church. A pastor speaks from the Word of God to his people only to hear them say 'But…!' How very hard it is for us simply to accept the Word of God without offering some sort of rebuttal!

This would be a sad and depressing situation indeed if it were not for the third speaker in these verses. This speaker is the Lord himself. How very kind he is to his people! He speaks tenderly to them in the midst of their doubt. He offers them assurance of his concern for them even though they had shown that they did not deserve it.

The loving mother

What does the Lord say to them? He argues from the lesser to the greater, from what is generally true to something that is unfailingly true. He says:

> 'Can a woman forget her nursing child,
> And not have compassion on the son of her womb?'
> (v. 15).

We know the answer to this question. It is generally true that mothers will not abandon their babies. But the Lord was not satisfied to assure his people on this general basis. If he had done so, someone would have been quick to cite an instance in which a mother did indeed abandon her child. We all know of many such instances today. The Lord, therefore, added this word:

> 'Surely they may forget,
> Yet I will not forget you'
> (v. 15).

We have, then, a solemn pledge from God himself that he would not abandon his people. Alexander Maclaren writes: 'There is more than a mother's love in the Father's heart.'[1]

The engraved hands

Not content to leave it there, the Lord added yet another
emblem or figure. He says:

'See, I have inscribed you on the palms of my hands...'
                                                    (v. 16).

In those days it was common practice for worshippers to in-
scribe the name of their god somewhere on their flesh. This
was evidently their way of showing how important their god
was to them. But here God tells his people that he has written
them on the palms of his hands.

This is a particularly powerful assurance, especially due to
the nature of the term God used. It is not mere writing, which
can be erased, but rather engraving. It is also most powerful
when we consider those to whom it was addressed, namely,
captives in Babylon. And why were they there? Because of
their sins! So here — wonderful thought! — is God saying to
these very captives that not even their sins could make him
forget them! Maclaren says, 'Let us neither be puzzled by our
sorrows nor made less confident when we think of our sins.
For there is no sin that is strong enough to chill the divine
love, or to erase us from the divine remembrance.'[2]

Simon Peter would come to rejoice in this truth. He failed
— and failed miserably. Three times he denied knowing our
Lord. But the Lord Jesus Christ pursued his failed disciple and
restored him to fellowship with himself. Even those black de-
nials could not erase his name from the hand of the Lord.

How can we know this to be true? How can we know that
God has the names of his people engraved on his hands? The
hands of Jesus give us the answer. Those hands were nailed to

a Roman cross so that God could provide eternal salvation for his people. We may rest assured that he would never have allowed his Son's hands to be nailed there if it were not for the engraving on his own hands.

The cross of Christ proves that God will never forget his people. If he, God, was willing to go to this length to redeem us, so far as giving up his Son to an agonizing death on the cross, we should never allow ourselves to think that he will forget us. If we meant that much to him we can be confident that we still mean enough to him that he will never forsake us.

The ever-seen walls

God offers his people yet another assurance that he had not forgotten them. He says:

'Your walls are continually before me'

(v. 16).

What a surprising statement this was for those captives in Babylon! The walls of Jerusalem, to which the Lord was referring, were not standing. They were in ruins. The Babylonian army had completely destroyed them. But where they saw ruins, God saw walls!

Many of those captives would have been inclined to point to those ruins and say, 'There, you see, is absolute proof that God has forgotten us. If he had not forgotten us, the walls of Jerusalem would still be standing.'

But God looked at things differently. We might say those ruins represented the sins which caused his people to go into captivity. But the walls before God's eyes represented his purpose for them. Now here is a cheering truth: their sins, serious as they were, could not defeat God's purpose for them and his gracious work in them. The walls of Jerusalem could be demolished and ruined but God's purpose for them could never be.

How could they be assured of this? All they had to do was wait. In due time, God would release them from captivity, and those ruined walls would be rebuilt. That would prove beyond any shadow of doubt that God's purpose for them was still intact and moving forward.

Every child of God can find comfort and consolation here. We all know what it is to fail God. We know what it is to break his commandments and bring his chastisement into our lives. And the devil is always eager to hold our sins before our eyes and to make certain pronouncements about us. He is always pointing to the ruins. But God's purpose for us will not be thwarted by our failures. He who has begun his work in us will complete it (Phil. 1:6).

> *If someone feels in his heart the situation is hopeless, I say you are looking at the ruins of life, while God looks at the walls. You look at what you have been and you are conscious of awful failure, but bless the Lord, He sees you in Christ, as what He intends you to be. He sees you as what you long to be in your best moments. He sees you as what you will be when the grace of God has finished the task.*
>
> *Alan Redpath*, Faith for the Times[3]

Are your circumstances such that you feel God has abandoned and forgotten you? Let these marvellous verses speak to your heart. If you are a child of God, you may be sure that he has not forgotten you. He cannot. His love for you is greater than the natural love a mother has for her child. In eternity past, he inscribed your name on his hand — and in his book of life. He looks upon you and sees, not the ruins of your life, but his purpose for you. The feeling of his heart, the engraving on his hands, the view before his eyes — all tell you that you are not forgotten by God.

Things are not always as they appear. Your circumstances may be very difficult and hard to explain but you, child of God, must never explain them in terms of being forgotten by God. That can never be.

For your journal...

1. Have you ever felt forgotten and forsaken by God? What circumstances make you feel this way? Can you accept his promise that he will never forsake his children even though their situation seems to suggest otherwise?

2. Are you comforted by the thought of God seeing walls where his people saw ruins? How does this help you? Do you often dwell on the ruins created by sin while God dwells on his purpose of grace for you?

Isaiah 50:4-11

'The Lord GOD has given me
The tongue of the learned,
That I should know how to speak
A word in season to him who is weary.
He awakens me morning by morning,
He awakens my ear
To hear as the learned.
The Lord GOD has opened my ear;
And I was not rebellious,
Nor did I turn away.
I gave my back to those who struck me,
And my cheeks to those who plucked out the beard;
I did not hide my face from shame and spitting.

'For the Lord GOD will help me;
Therefore I will not be disgraced;
Therefore I have set my face like a flint,
And I know that I will not be ashamed.
He is near who justifies me;
Who will contend with me?
Let us stand together.
Who is my adversary?
Let him come near me.
Surely the Lord GOD will help me;

Who is he who will condemn me?
Indeed they will all grow old like a garment;
The moth will eat them up.

'Who among you fears the LORD?
Who obeys the voice of his Servant?
Who walks in darkness
And has no light?
Let him trust in the name of the LORD
And rely upon his God.
Look, all you who kindle a fire,
Who encircle yourselves with sparks:
Walk in the light of your fire and in the sparks you have
    kindled —
This you shall have from my hand:
You shall lie down in torment.'

Day 11
Hallelujah! What a Saviour!

- ♦ *Begin by reading Isaiah 50*
- ♦ *Pray about what you have read*
- ♦ *Make notes on what you think God is teaching you*
- ♦ *Read the following chapter*
- ♦ *Answer the questions in the section 'For your journal'*

Isaiah 50:4-11

The Bible is no ordinary book. It was written by men who were inspired and carried along by the Holy Spirit of God. The Holy Spirit's intent in this particular passage is not hard to discern. He wanted us to understand that these words came from the Lord Jesus Christ. We are to hear him speaking these words centuries before he came to this earth.

So here we are, hundreds of years before the first coming of the Lord Jesus Christ, and he is giving details about his ministry and his death. And what he says here was fulfilled to the last detail when he came. What a wonder Scripture is!

Join me now in listening to these words from the Lord Jesus. As we listen, let us marvel at what our Lord says and what a Saviour we have.

Christ speaking to the weary

First, we have a Saviour who knows how to speak to the weary
(v. 4). The Lord says:

> 'The Lord GOD has given me
> The tongue of the learned,
> That I should know how to speak
> A word in season to him who is weary.'

With these words our Lord was pledging that he would come
in the office of prophet. He would come to declare the truth
of God. We know from the Gospel accounts that he did this in
a most powerful and riveting way (Matt. 7:28-29; Luke 4:31-
32; John 7:46).

But here the Lord Jesus calls attention to one particular
part of his preaching ministry, that is, speaking words to the
weary. The word 'weary' conjures up a picture of one who is
carrying such a heavy load that he does not have the strength
to continue.

There are many times in our lives when we have to carry
burdens or loads. Some loads are relatively light and easy to
carry. Others are crushing. Are you carrying a crushing load?
The Lord Jesus has a word for you. For those who are burdened with the guilt of their sins, he says, 'Come to me, all
you who labour and are heavy laden, and I will give you rest'
(Matt. 11:28). There is forgiveness with Christ if you will but
come to him, confessing your sins and accepting his salvation.

For those who are crushed under the load of sorrow over
the loss of a believing loved one, the Lord Jesus says, 'I am the
resurrection and the life. He who believes in me, though he
may die, he shall live' (John 11:25).

For those who are staggering beneath the load of responsibility, the Lord Jesus says, 'I am with you always, even to the end of the age' (Matt. 28:20). We must, of course, remember that Jesus' words of comfort are found in the Scriptures. If we want these words to be ours, we must read and study the Word of God and also hear it preached and taught.

On and on we could go. No matter how heavy the load and how weary we are, the Lord Jesus has a word of comfort for us. Hallelujah! What a Saviour!

Christ enduring anguish for his people

As we continue to listen to Christ speaking in these verses, we also realize that we have in him a Saviour who endured unspeakable anguish on our behalf (v. 6). The Lord says:

'I gave my back to those who struck me,
And my cheeks to those who plucked out the beard;
I did not hide my face from shame and spitting.'

Can there be any doubt about the occasion to which these words refer? They take us to those hours immediately before our Lord was crucified. What atrocities he suffered! No one has ever suffered more!

After he was arrested and tried, the Lord Jesus was handed over to the Roman soldiers so they could 'prepare' him for crucifixion. This they did by scourging him, by plucking his beard and by spitting upon him.

The scourging was the most horrific imaginable. William Hendriksen explains: 'The Roman scourge consisted of a short wooden handle to which several thongs were attached, the ends equipped with pieces of lead or brass and with sharply pointed bits of bone. The stripes were laid especially (not always exclusively) on the victim's back, bared and bent. The body was at times torn and lacerated to such an extent that deep-seated veins and arteries — sometime even entrails and inner organs — were exposed. Such flogging, from which Roman citizens were exempt, often resulted in death.'[1]

The plucking of the beard was a way of expressing contempt for someone. It was used to humiliate. Albert Barnes writes: 'To do this was to offer the highest insult that could be imagined among the Orientals. The beard is suffered to grow long, and is regarded as a mark of honour. Nothing is regarded as more infamous than to cut it off ... or to pluck it out; and there is nothing which an Oriental will sooner resent than an insult offered to his beard.'[2] Spitting in the face also expressed contempt. Barnes calls it 'an expression of the highest insult and indignity'.[3]

In our passage the Lord Jesus speaks of these things, and he actually experienced them when he came. Why did he allow himself to be so humiliated, to be treated with such indignity and contempt? Why did he go from the scourging, the plucking of his beard and receiving spit in his face to actually die in anguish and pain on the cross? He did it all for us. He endured such shame and humiliation in order to save us from our sins. These things did not just happen to him. No, he 'gave' his back and cheeks to his tormentors (v. 6). He was willing to go through all this for us. Hallelujah! What a Saviour!

Christ working in association with the Father

As we listen again to Christ speaking in the verses before us, we also realize that we have a Saviour who performed the work of redemption in the closest association with the Father and with complete dependence upon him. Where did the Lord Jesus get his words for the weary? He says:

'The Lord GOD has given me
The tongue of the learned...
The Lord GOD has opened my ear;
And I was not rebellious,
Nor did I turn away'

(vv. 4, 5).

And how did he face the humiliation and pain during the hours both before and while he was on the cross? He answers:

'For the Lord GOD will help me;
Therefore I will not be disgraced...
He is near who justifies me...
Surely the Lord GOD will help me'

(vv. 7, 8, 9).

We will never understand the great mysteries surrounding the doctrine of the Trinity. We know that God the Father, God the Son and God the Holy Spirit are each fully God. But we can also speak, as many theologians do, of the 'Economic Trinity'. This means that the three persons of the Godhead, while equal in every respect, took various roles in order to work out the plan of redemption. This required the second person of the Trinity, the Son of God, to take a subservient position to the Father. That is why we find him here speaking of learning from God and looking to God for help. Because the Lord Jesus lived in complete dependence upon the Father, he was given both the words of comfort that characterized his ministry and the strength to face his sufferings.

He who was not subservient by nature became subservient in order to save us. Because of his willingness to do this, God has justified (v. 8), or vindicated, him by raising him from the dead. Hallelujah! What a Saviour!

We have in Christ, then, one who speaks God's words, one who suffered in the place of sinners and who gladly submitted to the Father. And now we are all faced with the choice that is presented in the last two verses of this chapter. We can either rest upon the redeeming work of Christ (v. 10) or we can 'kindle' our own fire (v. 11), that is, form our own plan of salvation. The latter is the choice many are making these days, but it is a tragic choice indeed because God has promised that those who make it will finally 'lie down in torment' (v. 11).

> *Those that make the world their comfort, and their own right-eousness their confidence, will certainly meet with a fatal disappointment, which will be bitterness in the end. A godly man's way may be melancholy, but his end shall be peace and everlasting light. A wicked man's way may be pleasant, but his end and endless abode will be utter darkness.*
>
> *Matthew Henry,* Matthew Henry's Commentary[4]

For your journal...

1. Is it a comfort to you to know that the Lord Jesus speaks to his weary people? Do you agree that we find comfort in his words in Scripture? Write down some passages that you regard as particularly special instances of the Lord speaking to you.

2. Describe what the prophecy of Jesus' incredible suffering means to you.

Isaiah 51:11

*So the ransomed of the L*ORD* shall return,*
And come to Zion with singing,
With everlasting joy on their heads.
They shall obtain joy and gladness;
Sorrow and sighing shall flee away.

Day 12
Marching to Zion

♦ *Begin by reading Isaiah 51*
♦ *Pray about what you have read*
♦ *Make notes on what you think God is teaching you*
♦ *Read the following chapter*
♦ *Answer the questions in the section 'For your journal'*

Isaiah 51:11

Many old hymnals contain a gnarled selection entitled 'We're marching to Zion'. This hymn has fallen into the category of the little known and little appreciated. I cannot help but think that such hymns are falling into disuse, not because there is any flaw in them, but because there is a deep flaw in us. We do not understand them and, therefore, we do not like them. And here is our flaw: we do not understand these hymns because we do not understand the Scriptures.

The verses of 'We're marching to Zion' were written by Isaac Watts, and the chorus, added years later, was contributed by Dr Robert Lowry. This hymn is based squarely on the verse before us. If we can come to a better understanding of this verse, we will come to a better understanding of this hymn and appreciate it more fully. Let us think, therefore, about this idea of marching to Zion.

We must first establish the meaning of Zion. The name 'Zion' was first used in the account of David's conquest of the city of Jerusalem (2 Sam. 5:6-10; 1 Chron. 11:4-9). Some scholars think the word originally referred to a mountainous ridge and came to be applied to Jerusalem because it was located in a mountainous region.

Whatever the original meaning of the term, it was soon adopted as a nickname for the city of Jerusalem. It is also used by the biblical authors to designate the temple built by Solomon (Ps. 2:6; 48:2; 84:7; 132:13) and to the whole nation Judah (Isa. 1:27). Eventually it came, of course, to be applied to the new Jerusalem or heaven itself (Heb. 12:22; Rev. 14:1).

Scripture often moves on more than one level; that is, there is more than one level of legitimate interpretation. This is the case with the words of our text. On the basic or primary level, it quite clearly describes the return of the captives in Babylon to their homeland. These people would be ransomed or delivered from their captivity after seventy long years there and would return to Jerusalem with singing and much rejoicing.

The secondary and higher level of interpretation is that which is so wonderfully expressed by the hymn 'We're marching to Zion', namely, that it is a picture of the people of God on their way to their heavenly home. In other words, the first level, the Jews journeying from captivity in Babylon to their homeland in Judah, can be taken as a picture of the people of God journeying to heaven.

With this basic picture in mind, let us think about three things: our deliverance, our destination and the journey itself.

Our deliverance

The difficulty of the Jews' years of captivity is set forth by one of the psalmists:

> By the rivers of Babylon,
> There we sat down, yea, we wept
> When we remembered Zion.
> We hung our harps
> Upon the willows in the midst of it.
> For those who carried us away captive asked of us a song.
> And those who plundered us requested mirth,
> Saying, 'Sing us one of the songs of Zion!'
> How shall we sing the LORD's song
> In a foreign land?
>
> (Ps. 137:1-4).

But the Lord did not leave his people in captivity. He delivered or ransomed them, and there could be no doubt that it was he who did the delivering. He removed the Babylonians from the stage of world domination and put the Persians there instead. Then he worked in the heart of King Cyrus of Persia to write a decree of deliverance (Isaiah 44:28; 45:1-3).

All of this finds parallels in the experience of God's people. We came into this world in a state of captivity. We were born in sin and under Satan's dominion. We were alienated from God and bound for destruction. But just as God delivered the Jews from their political bondage in Babylon so he has delivered each child of God from spiritual bondage to Satan. The apostle Paul writes: 'He has delivered us from the power of darkness and conveyed us into the kingdom of the Son of his love' (Col. 1:13).

The apostle Paul's word 'conveyed' in Colossians 1:13 refers to removing people from one country and settling them in another. How great is salvation? It amounts to nothing less than a transfer of kingdoms. It takes us out of Satan's kingdom and resettles us as citizens in God's kingdom. That is great!

And there can be no doubt at all that God alone should receive the credit for effecting our deliverance. The Jews were not delivered from Babylon because they utilized some political clout. They had none to use. They were not delivered because they signed a petition. They were delivered because God managed events on the world stage to bring it about.

In the same way, we were not delivered from Satan because we possessed some power that intimidated him or because we signed a petition to persuade him. It came about because God did it for us. And we know what he did. He sent his Son to this world in our humanity, and Jesus broke Satan's hold on us. He did so by perfectly keeping the law of God on our behalf and by receiving in our stead the wrath of God.

Our destination

As the Jews were delivered from Babylon so that they could return to their homeland, so God has delivered us from Satan in order to bring us home to himself in heaven. We were rightfully his, but we were alienated from him through sin. Through his redeeming work in Christ, God has broken the chains of sin's bondage.

While we were in bondage, we were headed for eternal destruction. We had condemnation written all over us, but

God has changed our destination. Our reservation in hell has been cancelled and a place has been reserved for us in heaven.

God has only given us a few faint details, but what details! We will be living in a new city on a new earth, and there will be no sorrow, no pain, no weeping and no death (Rev. 21:1-4). There the words of our text will finally and fully be realized:

They shall obtain joy and gladness;
Sorrow and sighing shall flee away.

The journey

We believers have indescribable glory awaiting us, but we are not there yet. We are out of captivity, but we are not home. As the Jews had to journey from Babylon to their homeland, so we must journey from our captivity in sin to our home in heaven.

The journey from Babylon to Jerusalem posed no small challenge. There were wide expanses of barren, arid land. There were threats from wild beasts and thieves. We can also be sure that there was the hindrance of having to journey with complainers. The journey was long, arduous and very weary-ing. But despite all the challenges they would meet on the way, the returning captives would rejoice greatly. Isaiah says they would come to Zion 'with singing' and with 'everlasting joy on their heads'. Yes, they would 'obtain joy and gladness' once they arrived back in their land, but they would rejoice while they were actually completing the journey.

Our journey is also very challenging. Our release from Satan does not mean that he has gone away. He was once our master and now he is our enemy. He constantly seeks to defeat us as we travel along.

Some of our travelling companions are also complainers. They pull us down as we journey along. The journey for most of us is long, and we often find ourselves discouraged and weary. But in the midst of it all, we rejoice. We know that because Satan is a defeated foe, he can do us no real harm. And we know that the trials and difficulties we encounter are only temporary. We also rejoice because the Lord himself is with us. As Isaac Watts says, 'We're marching through Immanuel's ground.' Immanuel means 'God with us', and we may rest assured that he is indeed with us throughout our journey here. How do we know this? He sent the Lord Jesus Christ to this earth in our humanity. God would never have come among us in the first place if he intended to abandon us later in our journey.

Our past captivity and our future home have a transform-ing effect on the journey. No matter how difficult the journey is, it is never as bad as our captivity was. All that we encoun-ter and endure cannot begin to compare with the glory that will be ours. The apostle Paul put it like this: 'For our light affliction, which is but for a moment, is working for us a far more exceeding and eternal weight of glory, while we do not look at the things which are seen, but at the things which are not seen. For the things which are seen are temporary, but the things which are not seen are eternal' (2 Cor. 4:17-18).

So let us travel along rejoicing in the deliverance of our God, in the sure knowledge that, as we do, we will have even more to rejoice about in the future.

Let those refuse to sing who never knew our God,
But children of the heavenly King,
But children of the heavenly King,
May speak their joys abroad,
May speak their joys abroad.

...

Then let our songs abound
And every tear be dry;
We're marching through Immanuel's ground,
We're marching through Immanuel's ground,
To fairer worlds on high,
To fairer worlds on high.

(Isaac Watts)

For your journal...

1. Go through a hymnal. Write down the titles of other hymns that present the Christian life as a journey or pilgrimage. Write down phrases from these hymns that you find especially meaningful.

2. If we are to journey from this world to heaven, we must travel through 'Immanuel's ground'. Write down your thoughts on why Christ alone is the way of salvation.

3. Describe your response to the phrase 'Let those refuse to sing who never knew our God'.

Isaiah 52:7-8

*How beautiful upon the mountains
Are the feet of him who brings good news,
Who proclaims peace,
Who brings glad tidings of good things,
Who proclaims salvation,
Who says to Zion,
'Your God reigns!'
Your watchmen shall lift up their voices,
With their voices they shall sing together;
For they shall see eye to eye
When the L*ord* brings back Zion.*

Day 13
The joyous reception of a joyous proclamation

♦ *Begin by reading Isaiah 52*
♦ *Pray about what you have read*
♦ *Make notes on what you think God is teaching you*
♦ *Read the following chapter*
♦ *Answer the questions in the section 'For your journal'*

Isaiah 52:7-8

The prophet Jeremiah had been very clear. The people of Judah would be in captivity in Babylon for a seventy-year period (Jer. 25:11). As that period drew to a close, excitement began to build among the captives themselves and among the few people living around the ruins of Jerusalem. Those people, according to their custom, had watchmen posted by day and by night. From their high vantage point, these watchmen could see the approach of an enemy or messengers bearing important news.

One day a watchmen was scanning the horizon. He suddenly saw a lone figure coming towards him and the people.

The man was quite obviously carrying an important message. The watchman alerted the people, who dropped what they were doing and gathered together. In a few moments the runner arrived, and then they heard the good news. The captivity was over and many of the captives were even then on their way back to Jerusalem to rebuild the city and their homes.

What a celebration they must have had! They swarmed around the messenger to hug and kiss him. And, in the midst of the celebration, someone pointed to his feet and said, 'You have the most beautiful feet I have ever seen!' And they all laughed. Everyone understood. The messenger's feet had carried him to the ruins of Jerusalem to announce the best news these people could ever hear. Those feet were not beautiful in and of themselves, but in this particular situation they were beautiful beyond compare.

Let us think of it in this way. Suppose you are acquainted with a man who is perfectly likeable in every way but is extremely ugly. One day you are involved in a car accident. The doors are jammed, and it appears that the car will explode at any moment. Suddenly your ugly friend appears. He peers through the window with that ugly face and then pries open a door and frees you. Would you not tell it all around that his ugly face was the most beautiful sight you had ever seen?

In his letter to the Christians in Rome, the apostle Paul unfolds layer after layer of the gospel of Jesus Christ. When he comes to what we know as his tenth chapter, he again goes into detail about the Lord Jesus Christ providing for sinners the righteousness God demands and how God delivers this message of righteousness through the preaching of his Word. At this point Paul seizes the words we have here in Isaiah:

'How beautiful are the feet of those who preach the gospel
   of peace,
Who bring glad tidings of good things!'
(Rom. 10:15).

The gospel message of the preacher is so glorious that we must
bless the feet that carry him to the place where he can deliver
it.

And what is the gospel message? What makes it so glorious? Yes, it is, as Isaiah says, a message of good things and a
message of salvation. But our text allows us to see some of the
particular details about it.

Peace

The captives never knew real, genuine peace in Babylon. Their
hearts were always in Jerusalem, and they were always yearn-
ing to go back. But now they were returning home where they
would find peace.

The Bible is a message about peace broken and peace
restored. When God made Adam and Eve and placed them in
the Garden of Eden, they were at peace with him. He enjoyed
fellowship with them and they with him. But that idyllic scene
of peace was fractured when they disobeyed God. They now
sought to hide from God.

God could have left Adam and Eve with their sin and its
consequences. But he is a peace-loving and a peace-making
God. So he announced to Adam and Eve the plan of salvation
that he had already formulated. In that plan, the second person
of the Trinity, the eternal Son of God, would come to this

earth in human flesh. He would restore sinners to peace with God by taking their sin out of the way, and he would do this by receiving the penalty for it himself. When that penalty was paid, God was satisfied and peace was restored.

There is nothing worse in this life than to be at odds with God; and if we are at odds with God all through this life, we will be at odds with him in the world to come. But the gospel offers peace. It tells us that we do not have to be in conflict with him. Those who turn from their sins and trust in the Lord Jesus Christ alone as Lord and Saviour are delivered from their sins and are at peace with God. The apostle Paul says, 'Therefore, having been justified by faith, we have peace with God through our Lord Jesus Christ…' (Rom. 5:1).

Then our text also shows us that the gospel has another aspect.

The triumph of God

The messenger came bearing the news of the captives' release from Babylon. When he announced this message to the people of Jerusalem, they heard another message as well. As he spoke about the release, the inhabitants of Jerusalem may well have responded along this line: 'He is telling us that our God really does reign' (v. 7). The end of the captivity was to them indisputable and inescapable proof of the reign of God.

It must often have seemed to both the captives and the handful of people left around Jerusalem that God's reign was in doubt. They may often have thought that the Babylonians were in control, or even the devil himself, but certainly not God.

The captivity was not, however, a defeat for God. It was exactly the opposite. The people went into captivity because God brought it to pass. They had rebelled against God and his laws and had refused to heed his warnings. They stayed there in captivity until the time that God had designated. And when that time arrived, God so arranged events, pulling down the Babylonians and elevating the Persians, that his people were released.

Nothing had caught God by surprise and nothing had thrown him off course. Through it all and in it all, God was at work, achieving his purpose. Now as the people heard the glad message of the release, this truth hit home. God was indeed reigning.

The whole of human history is such that often it has looked as if God and his cause had come to utter defeat. It looked that way in the Garden of Eden when Satan tempted Adam and Eve. It looked that way again when Cain killed his brother Abel. It seemed to be the case when the earth's population became so corrupt that God sent the flood.

It often looked that way concerning God's promises about the Messiah coming through the nation of Israel, the tribe of Judah and the house of David. How Satan assailed each one! There were many times when it appeared that all would perish, and the promise of the Messiah would fall to the ground. But all the forces of hell could not defeat God, and the Messiah came at precisely the time he had determined. When the Lord Jesus Christ stepped on the stage of human history, Satan pulled out all the stops to defeat him, but Jesus stayed true to his course.

When Jesus died on the cross, it seemed as if Satan had at last succeeded and that God was finally defeated. But that cross, on which Jesus suffered untold agony and anguish, proved to be the supreme proof of God's reign. Satan's apparent victory was in reality his crushing defeat. His only victory at Calvary was bruising the heel of Christ. But that bruised heel came down with force upon Satan's head to deal the death blow to him and his kingdom (Gen. 3:15; Col. 2:15).

On all those occasions when God's cause looked to be dangling by a thread, it was in fact secure because the sovereign, almighty God was holding that thread.

> *When the enemies of the church have done their utmost, and seem to have gained their point; when they have overthrown the church, so that its being is scarcely visible, but is like a living root hid under ground; there is in it a secret life that will cause it to flourish again, and take root downward and bear fruit upward.*
>   *Jonathan Edwards,* The Works of Jonathan Edwards[1]

The captives of Babylon were on their way home and the people of Jerusalem would rejoice as they saw 'eye to eye' (v. 8), that is, up close. Those who know the Lord have just as many and more reasons to rejoice as they had. We have been restored to peace with God through the gospel. Our God has always reigned and will continue to reign throughout human history. And, best of all, we will eventually be able to see his reign up close.

What a gospel we have! How very thankful we should be for it! And how thankful we should be for those who faithfully proclaim it!

For your journal...

1. Do you believe that you place as high a value as you should on gospel ministers? Write down ways in which you can truly show your appreciation for them.

2. How do you respond to the emphasis of this chapter on the triumph of God? What conditions in our world cause you to feel discouraged? Write down any promises of God that help you to defeat discouragement.

Isaiah 53:4-6

Surely he has borne our griefs
And carried our sorrows;
Yet we esteemed him stricken,
Smitten by God, and afflicted.
But he was wounded for our transgressions,
He was bruised for our iniquities;
The chastisement for our peace was upon him,
And by his stripes we are healed.
All we like sheep have gone astray;
We have turned, every one, to his own way;
*And the L*ORD *has laid on him the iniquity of us all.*

Day 14
An amazingly detailed preview of Christ

♦ *Begin by reading Isaiah 53*
♦ *Pray about what you have read*
♦ *Make notes on what you think God is teaching you*
♦ *Read the following chapter*
♦ *Answer the questions in the section 'For your journal'*

Isaiah 53

If the promises of the cross as stated by the prophets could be considered to be a mountain range, this chapter is the Mount Everest of that range. Eight of its twelve verses are quoted in the New Testament in connection with the Lord Jesus Christ (vv. 1, 4, 5, 6, 7, 8, 9, 11), and his fulfilment of these prophecies is easily demonstrated. Consider the following details of the prophecy. Isaiah says the Messiah would:

• be wounded for our transgressions, bruised for our iniquities and receive 'stripes' for our healing (v. 5)
• be silent before his accusers (v. 7)

- be buried in a rich man's tomb (v. 9)
- be innocent of any wrongdoing (v. 9)
- be numbered with transgressors (v. 12)
- make intercession for transgressors (v. 12)
- be smitten by God, who would lay our iniquities upon him (v. 6), and bruise him (v. 10). All of these things would be in keeping with God's plan.

The writers of the New Testament vigorously assert and affirm that each of these prophecies found its fulfilment in Christ.

- Peter says the Lord Jesus 'bore our sins in his own body on the tree' and then specifically quotes Isaiah's phrase: 'by whose stripes you were healed' (1 Peter 2:24).
- Matthew specifically states that Jesus was silent before his accusers (Matt. 26:63).
- Matthew points out that Jesus was indeed buried in the tomb of a rich man (Matt. 27:57-60).
- Peter asserts that Jesus was innocent of any wrongdoing, and claims this to be a fulfilment of Isaiah's words (1 Peter 2:22).
- Mark declares that Jesus being crucified between two thieves is a fulfilment of Isaiah's prophecy that the Messiah would be numbered with the transgressors (Mark 15:28).
- Luke mentions that Jesus prayed for those who crucified him, an obvious fulfilment of Isaiah's claim that the Messiah would make intercession for transgressors (Luke 23:34).
- Jesus himself asserted on numerous occasions that all he did was in keeping with the plan of God (John 5:30; 8:42; 18:11).

This much loved chapter lends itself to a threefold division: the life of Christ (vv. 1-3), his death (vv. 4-10), and the results of his death (vv. 10-12). The major part of it, however, is devoted to his death on the cross.

> ...*the main business of the prophets was to point out Christ and his redemption. They were all forerunners of the great prophet. The main end why the spirit of prophecy was given them was that they might give testimony to Jesus Christ, the great Redeemer, who was to come... Some of them are very particular and full in their predictions of these things, and above all the prophet Isaiah, who is therefore deservedly called the evangelical prophet. He seems to teach the glorious doctrines of the gospel almost as plainly as the apostles did... How plainly and fully does the prophet Isaiah describe the manner and circumstances, the nature and end, of the sufferings and sacrifice of Christ, in the 53rd chapter of his prophecy! There is scarce a chapter in the New Testament itself which is more full upon it.*
>
> *Jonathan Edwards,* The Works of Jonathan Edwards[1]

In dealing with this matter, Isaiah's prophecy sounds many of the same notes as Psalm 22. What Christ was to suffer, and why, are common to both passages. How Christ was to suffer, that is, with what spirit he suffered, may also be found in both passages, but is stated more explicitly in Isaiah 53.

What Christ suffered

In his description of the Messiah's death on the cross, Isaiah resorts to a whole catalogue of words that are so keen and graphic they almost make us wince as we read them:

- wounded (v. 5) — pierced through, deeply and mortally hurt
- bruised (v. 5) — crushed or broken
- chastised (v. 5) — punished
- striped (v. 5) — struck with blows that opened the flesh
- oppressed (v. 7) — treated harshly with great hostility
- afflicted (v. 7) — abused
- taken from prison and judgement (v. 8) — quickly torn away from due process and hastened to death
- cut off (v. 8) — his life was rudely, violently and abruptly brought to an end
- stricken (v. 8) — struck violently

In addition to these gritty terms this question is posed: 'And who will declare his generation?'(v. 8). The upshot of this question is that no one in his generation, that is, no one among his contemporaries, would speak up in defence of him.

The city of Jerusalem suffered extreme hardship when she was invaded by Babylon and her citizens were either killed or deported. The prophet Jeremiah personified that suffering by imagining the city speaking for herself. Here is what she said:

> 'Behold and see
> If there is any sorrow like my sorrow,
> Which has been brought on me,
> Which the LORD has inflicted
> In the day of his fierce anger'
>
> (Lam. 1:12).

Had we been there to see the suffering of Jerusalem at that time we would certainly have found ourselves in agreement with her. There was no sorrow like her sorrow. That may even have remained true until Jesus came and suffered on the cross; but then it changed. The sorrow and suffering of Jesus on the cross far outstripped anything that the city of Jerusalem had experienced. No one has ever suffered what he suffered.

Why Christ suffered

Why did Christ have to suffer such untold agony and anguish on the cross? Isaiah 53 gives us the answer. It tells us that the Christ would not die as others do. His death would have the significance no other death in all of human history would have. It was to be a death for others, a death in which he took the place of others and bore their penalty.

The repeated use of the pronoun 'our' and the preposition 'for' tells us that Jesus would not die for his own sins, but rather for the sins of his people. It was 'our griefs' and 'our sorrows' that he carried with him to the cross. And it was 'for our transgressions', 'for our iniquities' and 'for our peace' that he died (vv. 4-5).

Why was it necessary for him to become the substitute for sinners and die in their stead? It was so they might go free. It all comes down to one thing. If Christ had not died for sinners, those sinners would have to die for themselves. If he had not experienced on the cross the full extent of God's wrath, those for whom he died would have to experience it themselves. But he *did* experience it, and now there is no wrath left for all those who know him.

We must note that this act of substitution was not something the Son did in isolation from the Father. The Father and the Son were not divided about the cross. The Lord Jesus did not go there to wring forgiveness out of an unwilling God. It was God the Father who 'laid' on Jesus 'the iniquity of us all' (v. 6). It was God the Father who was 'pleased' to 'bruise' him (v. 10). It was God the Father who 'put' him to grief (v. 10) and who would 'make' his soul 'an offering for sin' (v. 10).

It is also crucial for us to realize that the only way Jesus could become the substitute for others is if he had no sins of his own. If Christ had been guilty of so much as a single sin, he would have had to pay for his own sin and could not, therefore, have paid for the sins of others. Even this dimension of Christ's atoning death is not excluded from Isaiah's prophecy. He says of Christ, 'He had done no violence, nor was any deceit in his mouth' (v. 9).

How Christ suffered

Isaiah's amazingly detailed description of the cross does not end with what and why the Christ would suffer. It also unfolds the spirit with which he would suffer. Isaiah puts it like this:

> He was oppressed and he was afflicted,
> Yet he opened not his mouth;
> He was led as a lamb to the slaughter,
> And as a sheep before its shearers is silent,
> So he opened not his mouth
>
> (v. 7).

Christ went to the cross, not with a grudging obedience that could not find any way to avoid it, but with a glad and ready willingness. During his public ministry, he constantly empha-sized that he had come to do the Father's will, and that will carried him all the way to the cross. Even when the cross was scant hours away, he was able to say to the Father: '...your will be done' (Matt. 26:42).

The lamb before its shearers is indeed a most appropriate emblem for the willingness of Jesus to go to the cross. The lamb does not intimidate and frighten. It does not roar like a lion or strike rapidly like a snake. It is not able to sink its teeth deep into its enemies. It is completely defenceless against those who would harm it.

When Jesus stood before those who wanted to take his life, it was as a lamb. A lamb has no choice about being a lamb, but Jesus had a choice. He, as the eternal Son of God, could have called for 'twelve legions of angels' to utterly obliterate his crucifiers (Matt. 26:53), but he chose to be like a lamb and passively submit to the sufferings of the cross. How thank-ful we should be for that submission! Without it there would have been no way for us to escape the wrath of God.

It is worth noting that all Isaiah's descriptions of the cross are couched in the past tense. In other words, he speaks as though the event had already taken place, even though he lived more than seven hundred years before Christ. There is only one way to explain this. The Spirit of God had so drilled into Isaiah's spirit the certainty of that coming cross that Isaiah could speak of it as though it had already been accomplished.

We should rejoice in this great prophecy. Its fulfilment gives us proof that Scripture is the Word of God. It also means we have in Christ's redeeming death sure ground on which to stand when we face God.

For your journal...

1. How do you respond to Isaiah's description of the cross? Does the fact that it was so precisely fulfilled strengthen your faith? With the aid of a study Bible, write down other examples of fulfilled prophecy.

2. If Christ went ungrudgingly to the cross to die for undeserving sinners, does it not follow that we should ungrudgingly live for him? Can you say, as Paul did, that you are serving God with your spirit? (Rom. 1:9). Write down those things that seem to be keeping you from serving God in this way. What should you do about these things?

Isaiah 54:10, 17

'For the mountains shall depart
And the hills be removed,
But my kindness shall not depart from you,
Nor shall my covenant of peace be removed,'
Says the Lord, who has mercy on you.

…

'No weapon formed against you shall prosper,
And every tongue which rises against you in judgement
You shall condemn.
This is the heritage of the servants of the Lord,
And their righteousness is from me,'
Says the Lord.

Day 15
The immovable and
the unproductive

♦ *Begin by reading Isaiah 54*
♦ *Pray about what you have read*
♦ *Make notes on what you think God is teaching you*
♦ *Read the following chapter*
♦ *Answer the questions in the section 'For your journal'*

Isaiah 54:10, 17

The captives in Babylon would have found this particular chapter to be very comforting and consoling. Here the prophet assures them of future blessings. They were now few in number, but a day was coming when their tent would be greatly enlarged (vv. 1-3). They were now despised and oppressed, but a day was coming when their reproach would be forgotten (v. 4).

Such promises may very well have seemed too good to be true. These people were in captivity because they had sinned against the Lord and he had brought judgement upon them. What basis did they now have for believing that God could ever be merciful to them? The obstacles seemed to be so very large. What reason did they have to believe that they would be released and be able to rebuild their homeland?

In the verses before us the Lord addressed the concerns of his people by focusing their attention on the immovable and the unproductive.

The immovable

The Lord's words to these ancient people have immense value for us. We so often find ourselves depressed and despondent because our circumstances are difficult beyond measure. Much of our happiness lies in realizing what is immovable and what is unproductive. We so often get confused at this point. We find ourselves thinking that our circumstances are immovable and that the Lord's plans for us are unproductive.

This is not the case. Here is what is truly immovable in the lives of God's people — the kindness and mercy of the Lord. He says to these beleaguered captives:

'For the mountains shall depart
And the hills be removed,
But my kindness shall not depart from you…'

(v. 10).

We associate the mountains and hills with permanence. We gaze upon them in their lofty grandeur, and we think they will always stand. The Lord says his kindness towards his people is surer than the mountains and hills. They can be removed, but his kindness cannot.

Many of those captives would undoubtedly have been inclined to interpret their circumstances as evidence that God had not been kind to them. But that captivity, while it was indeed an expression of God's wrath and judgement, was also an expression of his kindness. It was intended, not for their destruction, but for their correction. The Lord says:

'For a mere moment I have forsaken you,
But with great mercies I will gather you.
With a little wrath I hid my face from you for a moment;
But with everlasting kindness I will have mercy on you...'
(vv. 7-8).

The captivity was not God's final word for his people. 'Everlasting kindness' was his final word. How could these people know this was the case? How could they be assured of God's everlasting kindness? How can we be assured of it? The answer is that the Lord has made with his people of all ages a 'covenant of peace' (v. 10). God has made a covenant with his people, and he always keeps his covenants.

The whole Bible is about God's covenant of peace with his people. God created Adam and Eve in his image, to live for his glory and, yes, to be his friends. But through sin, Adam and Eve broke their friendship with God and formed a friendship with Satan.

In his covenant of peace, which he had in place even before he created Adam and Eve, God pledged to restore Adam and Eve and all believers to friendship with himself. He accomplished this through the redeeming work of his Son, Jesus Christ. The Lord Jesus Christ restores peace between God and sinners by dealing with the cause of disrupted peace, that is, sin. On the cross, he received in his own person the penalty for sin. With sin's penalty paid, God is satisfied. There is no unresolved issue between himself and the believing sinner, and peace and friendship are restored.

We can rest assured that God would not put his Son through the excruciating agony of the cross if he intended to show only temporary mercy to his people. He put his Son through an eternity's worth of wrath on the cross because his mercy upon his people is eternal.

Mountains and hills will indeed pass away (2 Peter 3:10), but when they are nothing more than smouldering ashes God's mercy will still be in place. Our task is not to doubt that mercy when our circumstances are sour, but to believe that it is still in operation. Difficult times do not mean mercy has been withdrawn. The difficulties are part of his mercy. The fact that we have trouble understanding this does not make it any less true. That brings us to a further consideration.

The unproductive

How very often we who are God's people think that his plans and purposes are unproductive! It is not so! Here is what God himself says:

> 'No weapon formed against you shall prosper,
> And every tongue which rises against you in judgement
> You shall condemn'
>
> (v. 17).

The word 'weapon' takes us to the blacksmith's shop to view the forging of instruments that are intended to be used for attacking the church. The promise is that all such instruments, though they may appear effective for a while, will not finally prosper against the church.

The word 'tongue' takes us into the courtroom to hear a devastating verdict pronounced. The promise is that all human verdicts against the church will fail to stand. When the captives returned to their homeland, they indeed found many weapons trained on them and many voices raised in condemnation of them. The book of Nehemiah shows us the opposition they faced as they sought to rebuild the walls of Jerusalem. Although that opposition was very vigorous and determined, it failed.

The experiences of Nehemiah and his people were among the earliest in a long and continuous line of hatred for the church and opposition to her. The history of the church is largely the history of the devil sending out of the gates of hell every weapon imaginable for the destruction of the church. But the church sails on!

The history of the church is also the history of tongues rising up to condemn her, but she still sails on!

Argument, sophism, ridicule, have all been tried to overthrow the truth of the Christian religion. Appeals have been made to astronomy, geology, antiquities, history and indeed to almost every department of science, and with the same want of success. Poetry has lent the charm of its numbers; the grave historian has interwoven with the thread of his narrative covert attacks and sly insinuations against the Bible ... but thus far in all these contests ultimate victory has declared in favour of the Bible. And no matter from what quarter the attack has come, and no matter how much learning and talent have been evinced by the adversaries of the Bible, God has raised up some ... to meet these charges, and to turn the scales in favour of the cause of truth.

Albert Barnes, Notes on the Old Testament: Isaiah[1]

Victory over all forms of oppression and vindication from the Lord himself is the heritage of the church (v. 17). Albert Barnes writes: 'The inheritance which awaits those who serve God is truth and victory. It is not gold and the triumph of battle. It is not the laurel won in fields of blood. But it is the protection of God in all times of trouble; his friendship in all periods of adversity; complete victory in all contests with error and false systems of religion; and preservation when foes rise up in any form and endeavour to destroy the church, and to blot out its existence and its name.'[2]

What encouragement we have, then, in these verses! God's mercy upon his people is immovable and the enemies of the church will prove to be unproductive in the end. Let us rejoice in this. Our problems are not immovable, but God's mercy is. Our Lord is not unproductive, but our foes are.

For your journal...

1. We live in turbulent and uncertain days. Meditate on the immovable nature of God's mercy. Write down what this means to you and how it helps you.

2. Make a list of weapons that Satan is employing against the church today. Thank God for his promise that these weapons will not finally prevail.

Isaiah 55:6-9

*Seek the L*ORD* while he may be found,*
Call upon him while he is near.
Let the wicked forsake his way,
And the unrighteous man his thoughts;
*Let him return to the L*ORD*,*
And he will have mercy on him;
And to our God,
For he will abundantly pardon.

'For my thoughts are not your thoughts,
*Nor are your ways my ways,' says the L*ORD*.*
'For as the heavens are higher than the earth,
So are my ways higher than your ways,
And my thoughts than your thoughts.'

Day 16
Abundant pardon

- ♦ *Begin by reading Isaiah 55*
- ♦ *Pray about what you have read*
- ♦ *Make notes on what you think God is teaching you*
- ♦ *Read the following chapter*
- ♦ *Answer the questions in the section 'For your journal'*

Isaiah 55:6-9

Isaiah knew that the captives in Babylon would become keenly aware of the sins that caused them to go into captivity. He also knew that they would find themselves wondering if the seriousness of their sins had caused God's promises to be nullified.

Those captives would have found Isaiah's words in chapter 53 to be most encouraging and cheering. God's promise of the Messiah was still intact. They would also have been encouraged by the prophet's words in chapter 54. The people of God would flourish and grow in a remarkable way as a result of the Messiah's coming.

Having reassured the people of these things, the prophet turns his attention to yet another matter, that is, the individual

acceptance of the salvation the Messiah would come to provide. It was essential for the prophet to do this. He could not
allow his readers to think that it was sufficient for them merely
to be a part of the nation which had received the promise of
the Messiah. They were not saved just by being born into Israel.
The apostle Paul makes this abundantly clear with these words:
'...they are not all Israel who are of Israel, nor are they all
children because they are the seed of Abraham...' (Rom. 9:6-
7). In other words, each individual had to embrace the work
of the coming Messiah with a true and living faith. This chapter consists of God calling individuals to such faith. Derek
Thomas calls this chapter 'God's own gospel sermon'.[1]

What a breathtaking thought! God preaching to and pleading with us! The verses before us constitute the heart of this
sermon. We can divide these verses into four major parts: the
offer, the terms on which the pardon is granted, the need for
immediate action and the danger to be avoided.

The offer

This offer is conveyed to us in these words: '...our God ... will
abundantly pardon' (v. 7). We know what pardon is. A man
has committed murder. He is tried, found guilty and sentenced
to death by lethal injection. The day of his execution has
arrived, and he is taken from his cell to the death chamber.
Suddenly, the phone rings, and the caller announces that the
President has pardoned the man. Does the warden proceed
with the execution? Of course not. The man has been
pardoned. He has been released from the penalty of his
wrongdoing.

This is only a very faint representation of spiritual truths. The Bible tells us that we all without exception stand guilty before God. We have broken his laws, and he has sentenced us, as is his right, to eternal separation from himself. He could carry out this sentence, and no one could accuse him of being unjust or unfair.

But, wonder of wonders, the very God who has justly sentenced us now offers pardon, abundant pardon, to us. Why is it called abundant? Our sins are abundant, and the evil of our sins is abundant, so the pardon that releases us from them is abundant. It is more than sufficient for our sins.

> *The Lord Hungerford of Hatesby was beheaded in Henry VIII's time. The Lord Thomas Cromwell, a better man, but executed together with him, cheered him up and bade him be of good comfort; For, said he, if you repent, and be heartily sorry for that you have done, there is for you also mercy with the Lord, who, for Christ's sake, will forgive you; therefore be not dismayed.*
> *John Trapp*, Commentary on the Old & New Testaments[2]

The well-known hymn of Julia H. Johnston celebrates the abundant pardon that flows to us from the grace of God:

Grace, grace, God's grace,
Grace that will pardon and cleanse within;
Grace, grace, God's grace,
Grace that is greater than all our sin.

How is God able to offer this abundant pardon? He cannot do so by ignoring our sins. His holiness requires the penalty for sin to be paid. He is able to offer pardon on the basis that he poured out the penalty for sinners on his own Son, Jesus Christ. God only demands that the penalty for sins be paid once. And if Christ on the cross received the penalty for me, I will not have to pay that penalty.

Perhaps someone will ask where such teaching is found in this text. The answer is, of course, that the pardon of this fifty-fifth chapter flows from that which is described in the fifty-third chapter, namely, the redeeming, atoning death of the Messiah (note especially vv. 4-6 and vv. 10-12).

The terms

It is not enough for God in mercy to offer pardon for sinners. That pardon has to be received. Isaiah conveys this with the words 'seek', 'call', 'forsake' and 'return' (vv. 6-7).

Seek

'Seek' means we are to actively pursue God's pardon as we would pursue anything of surpassing value.

Call

'Call' means we are to cry out to God for the pardon. We are to sue him for his mercy.

Forsake and return

'Forsake' and 'return' present the two sides of repentance. On one hand, we are to forsake our sin. On the other hand, we are to turn to God. We are, in other words, to do an about-turn.

We have had our faces turned towards our sins and our backs towards God. If we desire to receive his pardon, we must now turn our backs towards sin and our faces towards him.

The need for immediate action

The Lord says:

> Seek the LORD while he may be found,
> Call upon him while he is near
>
> (v. 6).

These words are at one and the same time consoling and terrifying. They console us because they assure us that the Lord may be found and he is near.

God would be justified in keeping his distance from sinners for ever, but he comes near. He does so when his gospel is preached, and when we are reminded in any way of death. Such reminders come when death invades our circle of family or friends, or when we experience sickness or calamity. He also comes near when anyone speaks to us of our need of Christ.

These same words terrify us because they indicate that a time will come when the Lord will not be found and will not be near. The people of Noah's day found this to be so. For years, the ark Noah was building was very near and accessible. But there came a day when the door of the ark was shut and there was no escape from the flood (Gen. 7:16).

The rich man in Jesus' parable found it to be so. He lived his life without regard to God only to find himself in eternity separated from God by an unbridgeable chasm (Luke 16:19-31).

How very kind God is to plead patiently with sinners! But the day of pleading will give way to unrelenting justice. The same grace that now urges God to spare sinners a while longer will eventually side with justice and approve of the destruction of sinners (Luke 13:6-9).

The danger to be avoided

There is no difficulty identifying this danger. It is presented clearly in our text. The danger is thinking our own thoughts and following our own ways with regard to this matter of pardon. This is exactly what many are doing. They reject the pardon freely offered by God because they are filled with their own ways and thoughts. It is commonplace to hear someone say, 'I have my own ideas about religion.'

This may be the idea that all are destined to be saved regardless of what they do with Christ. Or it may be the idea that those who are generally pleasant and nice are certain to be saved. Perhaps it is the idea that those who belong to any kind of church are saved.

There is no shortage of ideas about salvation. It is a day in which each man's religion goes no farther than his own hat. Our age celebrates and dignifies such notions with the words 'pluralism' and 'tolerance', and scorns those who say there is only one way of salvation with such words as 'bigoted' and 'obscurantist'. Meanwhile God solemnly reminds us that his thoughts are not our thoughts and his ways are not our ways (vv. 8-9).

God's way of pardon is, as we have noted, through the redeeming work of his Son. His way of pardon is not to ignore sin but to judge sin. His way of pardon is that blood-stained cross outside Jerusalem that appears to be so very foolish to sophisticates. His way of pardon can only be received by faith in Christ. His way of pardon requires us to renounce our own thoughts and ways and submit to his, as he emphatically reminds us:

> There is a way that seems right to a man,
> But its end is the way of death
>
> (Prov. 16:25).

The course of wisdom, then, is to thank God that he has a way of pardon and to turn from our own thoughts and ways to embrace his. We do this only by renouncing every other hope for salvation and resting completely upon the saving work of the Lord Jesus Christ.

For your journal...

1. How do you respond to Derek Thomas' description of Isaiah 55 as 'God's own gospel sermon'? Think of this chapter as God speaking directly to you. Does this make the chapter more meaningful? Do you feel a sense of gratitude that God speaks to you in this way? What does God's speaking tell us about him?

2. Write down some of the thoughts modern men and women have about the matter of salvation. What parts of God's plan of salvation do many find to be objectionable?

Isaiah 56:8

*The Lord G*ᴏᴅ*, who gathers the outcasts of Israel, says,*
'Yet I will gather to him
Others besides those who are gathered to him.'

Day 17
Our gathering God

- *Begin by reading Isaiah 56*
- *Pray about what you have read*
- *Make notes on what you think God is teaching you*
- *Read the following chapter*
- *Answer the questions in the section 'For your journal'*

Isaiah 56:8

This is an extremely heart-warming text. It tells us something about God that we all need to know, namely, he is a gathering God. Here the Lord refers to himself as 'The Lord GOD who gathers'.

We can all think of people who divide and scatter. They are in our nation, our churches and our homes. Wherever they go, they leave fragments scattered here and there. There are times when the Lord has found it necessary to scatter. The people to whom this text was originally written had been scattered by God. He had driven them from their homeland, and they were now captives in Babylon. This was God's judgement upon them for stubbornly refusing to walk in the ways he had commanded them.

But while God had found it necessary to scatter his people in judgement, he did not delight in doing so. He calls judgement his 'unusual' or 'strange' work (Isa. 28:21). It was a work that gave him no pleasure. Gathering people — reaching out to scattered fragments and bringing them together — is the work in which God delights. He is the gathering God. He is the father who gathers in his arms the son that has strayed into the far country (Luke 15:20).

Let us look at this text so we can rejoice in our gathering God.

The ones whom God promises to gather

The outcasts of Israel

God first promises to gather 'the outcasts of Israel'. There is no difficulty here. The Lord was telling his people that captivity in Babylon would not be his final word for them. He would bring them back to their homeland. He explicitly promised this in these words:

'For a mere moment I have forsaken you,
But with great mercies I will gather you'
(Isa. 54:7).

The truth of God gathering his people from Babylon is wonderfully described in Ezekiel 37. There the Lord takes the prophet to a valley full of dry bones and asks him if those bones could live. The Lord then commands him to prophesy to the bones. The bones immediately come together and are covered with flesh. The corpses then stand up. Ezekiel is commanded to prophesy again, and this time the breath of life enters into the corpses.

Here is the explanation the Lord gave to Ezekiel for this strange episode:

> 'Son of man, these bones are the whole house of Israel. They indeed say, "Our bones are dry, our hope is lost, and we ourselves are cut off!" Therefore prophesy and say to them, "Thus says the Lord GOD: 'Behold, O my people, I will open your graves, and cause you to come up from your graves, and bring you into the land of Israel'"'
>
> (Ezek. 37:11-12).

This promise was fulfilled. The people of Israel were released from their captivity by Cyrus, King of Persia, after he conquered the Babylonians. Through this, God proved himself to be the gathering God.

'Others besides'

Yet there is more. In our text the Lord also promises to gather 'others besides'. This part of the promise tells us that God would include in his gathering some who were not part of Israel, and he would make them his own.

The first part of this fifty-sixth chapter of Isaiah deals with this very thing. The Lord speaks to 'the son of the foreigner who has joined himself to the LORD', that is, to a Gentile who possessed true faith in God (vv. 3, 6). He also addresses the eunuch, that is, one who could not father children (v. 3). The people of Israel believed such men were to be excluded from the privileges of the people of God. But our gathering God promises to reach out to them and bring them into the life of his people, and to do so in such a way that they need not feel any inferiority.

The promises God made to these outsiders has found abundant fulfilment in the countless multitudes of Gentiles who have come crowding into the kingdom of Christ. They are there because our gathering God has thrown open the doors of his kingdom, not to those who physically descended from Abraham, but rather to those who hold the faith of Abraham (John 8:39; Gal. 3:7-9).

> *The Lord Jesus promised to gather Gentiles into his kingdom with these words: 'And other sheep I have which are not of this fold; them also I must bring, and they will hear my voice; and there will be one flock and one shepherd' (John 10:16). These words led Charles Spurgeon to say: 'Our Shepherd-King has greater thoughts than the most large-hearted of his servants. He delights to enlarge the area of our love.'*
>
> *Charles Spurgeon,* Metropolitan Tabernacle Pulpit[1]

We come now to a second major consideration.

The basis on which God gathers his people

It is no small thing to speak of God gathering sinners unto himself. God is holy and demands perfect righteousness of us. We, on the other hand, are sinners without any righteousness at all to meet God's demand, and God cannot take sinful people unto himself in their sins. To do so would compromise his holy character.

The great question of the ages, then, is how God can gather sinners to himself. To put it another way, how can God at one and the same time maintain his holiness and yet forgive sinners? The prophecy of Isaiah and the whole Bible trumpet the answer. It is only through the Lord Jesus Christ.

Isaiah here mentions a covenant (v. 4). This takes us right to the very heart of the matter. The first person of the Trinity, that is, the Father, made a covenant or agreement with the second person of the Trinity, that is, the Son. In this agreement, the Son pledged to take upon himself our humanity. He had to do this because he could not truly represent us if he were not one of us. He further pledged that he would perfectly obey God's laws on our behalf, thus providing the righteousness God demands. He also pledged that he would go to Calvary's cross and there receive the penalty that our sins deserve. In short, the Lord Jesus Christ pledged to provide for us the righteousness we lack and to pay for the sins we possess. This and this alone is God's way of salvation. This is the way in which he gathers sinners unto himself.

But how does the redeeming work of the Lord Jesus Christ become ours? The answer, as it says in the Authorized Version, is that we must 'take hold' of what God has done for sinners in Christ. In other words, we must 'take hold' of this covenant that God the Father and God the Son made.

What does it mean to 'take hold' of God's covenant? Matthew Henry explains it in these terms: '...to take hold of it is to consent to it, to accept the offer and come up to the terms, deliberately and sincerely to take God to be to us a God and to give ourselves to him to be to him a people. Taking hold of the covenant denotes an entire and resolute consent to it, taking hold as those that are afraid of coming short, catching at it as a good bargain, and as those that are resolved never to let it go, for it is our life...'[2]

God has done everything necessary for sinners to be saved, and, in the wideness of his mercy, he invites sinners to come and receive what he has done. No one is too bad to come. God gathers outcasts to himself! But neither is anyone too good to come! All must come to God through the salvation he has provided in his Son. All are commanded to 'take hold' of the covenant of grace and rest upon it as their only hope for eternal salvation. All are required to come and all who come are received by our gathering God.

Have you come to Christ? Have you taken hold of him? Are you resting completely upon what he did for sinners? Do not be taken in by popular notions of our day that we are all automatically the children of God and all we must do to finally be received by him is die. Heed what the Lord Jesus himself said so emphatically, 'I am the way, the truth, and the life. No one comes to the Father except through me' (John 14:6).

How thankful we should be that God is a gathering God, and that he has through Christ made it possible for us to be gathered to him! Because God gathers sinners to himself, those who believe have a tremendously glorious future awaiting them. The Bible says that the God who gathers sinners to fellowship with himself in this life will eventually gather them into his own presence in heaven. That great throng will consist of saints from every tribe, tongue, people and nation (Rev. 5:9). And their glad song of praise will be:

> 'Blessing and honour and glory and power
> Be to him who sits on the throne,
> And to the Lamb, for ever and ever!'
>
> (Rev. 5:13).

For your journal...

1. Look through the four Gospels. Write down the names of any outcasts mentioned whom Jesus gathered unto himself.

2. Read Revelation 5. What is your response to its description of God gathering his people home? Be sure to thank God for his glorious salvation.

Isaiah 57:14-16

And one shall say,
'Heap it up! Heap it up!
Prepare the way,
Take the stumbling block out of the way of my people.'

For thus says the High and Lofty One
Who inhabits eternity, whose name is Holy:
'I dwell in the high and holy place,
With him who has a contrite and humble spirit,
To revive the spirit of the humble,
And to revive the heart of the contrite ones.
For I will not contend for ever,
Nor will I always be angry;
For the spirit would fail before me,
And the souls which I have made.'

Day 18
Reasons to believe and not doubt

♦ Begin by reading Isaiah 57
♦ Pray about what you have read
♦ Make notes on what you think God is teaching you
♦ Read the following chapter
♦ Answer the questions in the section 'For your journal'

Isaiah 57:14-16

In these verses the Lord assures his people once again that their captivity in Babylon would not be permanent. In due time they would be released and return to their own land. Having abandoned their idols and returned to trusting the Lord, the people would again 'possess the land' and 'inherit' God's holy mountain (v. 13), that is, the mountain on which their temple had been situated.

In those days, cities and villages would receive distinguished visitors by sending out a labour force to remove all stones and impediments in the road. God uses this imagery to promise that all the obstacles to their return home would be removed (v. 14).

These were certainly cheering promises. But it seems that God's people are never able to receive his promises without some of their number raising objections and doubts, or without doubts arising within their own hearts. We no sooner receive a glorious promise from God than we hear the voice of doubt whispering urgently, saying, perhaps, 'The promise is too good to be true'; or, 'The difficulties are too great.'

God was not content, therefore, merely to give his people this promise of their release from Babylon and their return home. He proceeds to tell them why they must believe in his promise.

Security is much on our minds these days. What a blessing it is to know that God's promises are totally secure!

The loftiness of God

One reason is that he, the giver of the promise, is the high and lofty God who inhabits eternity (v.15). By describing himself in this way, the Lord was essentially saying to his people, 'If you doubt my promise, think about who I am.'

What does it mean when God says he is high and lofty? It means he alone is God. He is above all others. He is the incomparable God. Matthew Henry says this phrase means '...his being and perfections are exalted infinitely above every creature, not only above what they have themselves, but above what they can conceive concerning him...'[1]

It is not hard to see how this phrase would have brought encouragement to the captives in Babylon. They had no short-age of excuses for doubting God's promise to bring them back to their land. The Babylonians were too strong. The journey home was too long and dangerous, and Jerusalem was in a desperate and hopeless condition.

The Babylonians *were* strong. The desert *was* dangerous. Jerusalem *was* desolate. But none of these circumstances was too great or too difficult for God. He is the high and lofty one.

- God is high and lofty in *glory*. There is no creature that can compare to him in majesty and splendour.
- God is lofty in *wisdom*. There is no problem too complex for him.
- God is high and lofty in *power*. There is nothing that can defeat him.

What does God mean when he says he inhabits eternity? We will be helped in our understanding of this by thinking first about ourselves. We are creatures of time. As we journey through this world, we are constantly puzzling over our circumstances and our calamities. What do they mean? Where will they lead? What will we do if this happens? What will we do if that happens?

We can well imagine the captives in Babylon doing the same. What a refreshing word it was for them to hear God say he inhabits eternity! God is not subject to time and all its twists and turns. He is not sitting in heaven trying to figure out his next move. He is not wondering what will happen next or where it will lead.

God is sovereign. He is not a captive to this temporal, passing world. He is above it all and in control of it all. He knows what he is doing. He knows the end that he appointed for all things, and he knows exactly how he will achieve that end.

His people in Babylon could very well have been inclined to respond to his promise to release them by saying, 'Lord, don't you know, we inhabit Babylon and Babylon is strong.' The Lord was essentially saying, 'My people, don't you know, I inhabit eternity, and it doesn't matter how strong Babylon is.'

> *He is a God, saith one, whose nature is majesty, whose place is immensity, whose time is eternity, whose life is sanctity, whose power is omnipotency, whose work is mercy, whose wrath is justice, whose throne is sublimity, whose seat is humility.*
> *John Trapp,* Commentary on the Old & New Testaments[2]

Because God inhabits eternity, all believers can joyfully sing with Henry F. Lyte:

> Change and decay in all around I see:
> O Thou who changest not, abide with me!

Another reason God's people should not doubt his promises is that his name is holy (v. 15).

The holiness of God's name

When God says his name is holy, he means he himself is holy, that is, morally perfect. His name stands for himself. He is a holy God.

What did this particular claim have to do with the issue at hand of whether the people of God could trust the promises of God? The answer is quite obvious. Because God has moral perfection it is impossible for him to lie. If he had given those captives a promise only to break it, he would no longer be a holy God.

This is just as important for us as it was for those captives. God has made promises to us, as well. He has promised to grant eternal life to all who believe. That promise is sure and secure because God, in the words of the apostle Paul, 'cannot lie' (Titus 1:2; see also Heb. 6:18).

Yet another reason God's people should not doubt God is his compassionate nature (Isaiah 57:15-16).

The compassionate nature of God

Now we come to the most cheering — and staggering — part of this promise. God is high and lofty. God inhabits eternity. God is holy. And now we read that God is concerned about his people. He dwells in heaven, but he also dwells 'with him who has a contrite and humble spirit' (v. 15).

We come now to the purpose behind the captivity. Why would God ever cause his people to go through such an agonizing experience? It was to humble them. God's people had become very proud and arrogant. He had blessed them with innumerable blessings, but they had turned their backs on him and sought after idols. God sent messenger after messenger to call them to repentance and warn them of judgement. But they had refused to heed.

After patiently enduring their rebellious ways for many years, the Lord did just as he promised. He brought the Babylonians upon them to destroy the city of Jerusalem and its beautiful temple, and to carry them away captive for a period of seventy years.

That period of captivity, severe as it was, reaped a very wonderful benefit, namely, causing the people to see the uselessness of their idols and preparing them to receive the renewed favour of God.

The captivity did indeed humble the people, and put them in a position to receive this incredibly good and glorious news from God:

'I dwell…
With him who has a contrite and humble spirit,
To revive the spirit of the humble,
And to revive the heart of the contrite ones'

(v. 15).

'In the lowest hearts he dwelleth, as well as in the highest heavens.
A broken heart is God's lesser heaven; here he dwelleth with
delight.'
    John Trapp, Commentary on the Old & New Testaments[3]

There is here a spiritual truth of immense value. If we want God to be near, we must be humble. Scripture says, 'God resists the proud, but gives grace to the humble' (James 4:6; 1 Peter 5:5).

This has application for those who are not Christians. If you want to be saved, you must humble yourself before God. How few are willing to do this! This is a day in which people are ever ready to fight with God. They are confronted with the Bible's message about sin and coming judgement, and they immediately begin to find fault with it. They hear that God's way of salvation is through his Son dying on a Roman cross, and they immediately dismiss it as absurd and ludicrous.

This is a day in which people are very sure and very proud of themselves. But there is no salvation for those who are concerned only with themselves and the latest trends. There is only salvation for those who come to the end of themselves and in humility bow before God to cry out: 'Lord, you are absolutely right about me and my sin, and your way of salvation is the only way.'

This truth also applies to believers. Although we have been saved, we can still become very proud of ourselves. When we do, we rob ourselves of God's blessings and invite his chastisement. But when we become sick of our proud and rebellious ways and turn from them, God will renew us because he delights 'to revive the spirit of the humble, and to revive the heart of the contrite ones'.

There was, therefore, absolutely no reason for the captives in Babylon to doubt God's promise to release them. He, the high and holy one who inhabits eternity and who cannot lie, has a tender compassion for his people. Because God has not changed, we his people today can also trust him to fulfil all his promises to us.

For your journal...

1. Read Isaiah 40:12-31 for more about the loftiness of God. What does this description mean to you? How does it help you?

2. Think about God humbling his people. Can you identify ways in which God has humbled you? Can you thank God for these instances?

Isaiah 58:9-12

'If you take away the yoke from your midst,
The pointing of the finger, and speaking wickedness,
If you extend your soul to the hungry
And satisfy the afflicted soul,
Then your light shall dawn in the darkness,
And your darkness shall be as the noonday.
The LORD will guide you continually,
And satisfy your soul in drought,
And strengthen your bones;
You shall be like a watered garden,
And like a spring of water, whose waters do not fail.
Those from among you
Shall build the old waste places;
You shall raise up the foundations of many generations;
And you shall be called the Repairer of the Breach,
The Restorer of Streets to Dwell In.'

Day 19
A promise of blessing and the pathway to blessing

- ♦ *Begin by reading Isaiah 58*
- ♦ *Pray about what you have read*
- ♦ *Make notes on what you think God is teaching you*
- ♦ *Read the following chapter*
- ♦ *Answer the questions in the section 'For your journal'*

Isaiah 58:9-12

As we have been noting all along, the last twenty-seven chapters of Isaiah were written for those Jews who would be taken captive by the Babylonians. Isaiah wrote these chapters over one hundred years before that captivity actually took place. He was enabled by the Spirit of God to write these messages in advance so the captives would find comfort in them while they were in Babylon.

The captives would have been particularly comforted by Isaiah's frequent assurance that they would eventually be released from their captivity and restored to their homeland.

The promise of blessing

Isaiah repeats that promise in the verses of our text. He does so in a very wonderful way, that is, by assuring the captives that they would be both the recipients and the means of blessing.

The recipients of blessings

Isaiah portrays the blessings they would receive in a delightful way. He says that a type of noonday light would 'dawn in the darkness' (v. 10), that is, the darkness of their adverse and difficult circumstances would give way to the light of prosperity and blessing. He assures them that the Lord would guide them continually (v. 11). They would not feel as if the Lord had utterly forsaken them and they had been left alone to find their own way through life's darkness.

Isaiah also promises that the Lord would satisfy their souls in drought (v. 11). Their spiritual barrenness would give way to a time of unusual spiritual vitality. They would receive 'showers of blessing'.

Then the prophet promises that the Lord would strengthen their bones (v. 11). God would give them support and strength even as the bones strengthen and support the body. He also tells them that the Lord would make them 'like a watered garden, and like a spring of water, whose waters do not fail' (v. 11). Matthew Henry understands this to mean they would be 'flourishing and fruitful in graces and comforts'.[1]

These represent very remarkable blessings indeed. But the prophet has even more to mention. In verse 12 he promises that the returning captives and their descendants would

rebuild their cities. They would, then, not only receive blessings but would be the means of bringing blessing upon the
whole nation.

The means of blessing

They would do so by rebuilding 'the old waste places', that is,
rebuilding those things that were in ruins. They would also
'raise up the foundations of many generations', that is, restore
or relay old foundations. They would be called 'the Repairer
of the Breach', that is, those who repaired the walls that were
broken down. They would also be called 'The Restorer of
Streets to Dwell In'. In other words, they would repair the
roads that led to their dwelling places. Matthew Henry sum-
marizes the details of verse 12 with these words: 'They and
their families shall be public blessings.'[2]

It should be immediately obvious that this passage has
pointed significance for us. So very often we are more concerned about being blessed than we are about being blessings.
We are more interested in receiving than in giving.

This is certainly a time in which God's people need to be
'public blessings'. Our churches do not lie in physical ruins as
the homeland of the captives did, but there is abundant evidence that many of them are in spiritual ruins. They were
once beautiful, but now they are 'waste places'. Many of the
foundations — the truths and principles on which they were
founded — have been broken down and lie in shambles. The
protecting wall of truth around the church has been breached
and the enemy pours in, while virtue and vitality pour out.

Because the churches are in such a dire and desperate condition, our society, our homes and individual lives suffer ruin

and devastation as well. Oh, that God's people would have a burden for the times and desire both to receive God's blessings and to channel them to others!

How is it possible for us to be both the recipients and the means of blessing? Isaiah tells us. He was not content merely to promise blessing, but also to make clear the pathway to blessing.

The pathway to blessing

The captives in Babylon were not assured of these blessings apart from their own hearty obedience to God. They were not entitled to sit down and say, 'If God has promised these things, there is nothing for us to do.'

We always have to fight the tendency to separate the end from the means; but God always keeps them together. If he has promised a certain end, he has promised certain means to reach that end, and we cannot have the one without the other.

What was the pathway for these captives to follow to reach the end that God had promised? What did they have to do in order to be both the recipients and the channel of those blessings? The first part of this fifty-eighth chapter of Isaiah enables us to answer that question in a very succinct way — they had to keep the fast that God had chosen (vv. 5, 6).

As we read the first portion of this chapter, we find the Lord commanding Isaiah to cry out against the sins of the people. Even while in captivity, they were far from God. They had turned away from their idols, but they were not truly serving God with their hearts. While they were fasting in order to secure the blessings of God, they were also oppressing their

'labourers' (perhaps their fellow-captives who were indebted
to them) and arguing with their neighbours (vv. 3-4).

*We are very good at separating or compartmentalizing things
that belong together. We think of the blessings of God on our
lives as being one compartment and wonder why God doesn't
bestow his blessings. We think of our own conduct as another
compartment that has nothing to do with the first. But God has
placed both his blessings and our conduct in the same compartment. We must not expect the former if we are not willing to
grant the latter.*

They were not to expect, then, that their fasting would secure
the blessing of God if they did not join to their fasting the
kind of behaviour that pleases God. And what kind of behaviour is that? God leaves no room for doubt about this. He calls
them to several duties:

- they must stop burdening others with oppressive burdens
  but learn to show mercy (vv. 6, 9).
- they must share with the needy (vv. 7, 10)
- they must stop hiding themselves from their own flesh
  (v. 7), that is, from their own family members. Apparently,
  they were either ashamed of their own family members who
  were poor and humble or they were depriving their family
  members of common necessities. Whatever they were doing
  in this area, they were to stop.
- they were to stop 'pointing the finger' (v. 9). They were to
  stop showing contempt and scorn for others.
- they were to stop 'speaking wickedness' (v. 9). They were
  to refrain from every kind of false, harsh, and unjust
  speaking.[3]

- they were also to stop regarding the Sabbath as their own day and honour it as God's holy day (v. 13).

Going through religious motions did not help the people during Isaiah's time, and it would not help the captives in Babylon. God is not impressed with a religion that does not come from the heart and does not shape and mould the life.

This is the point at which this passage speaks so very powerfully to us. We often fall into the trap of going through religious duties with our hearts not being right with God. We expect our performance of those duties to secure the blessing of God, but God is not pleased with the mere outward show. He wants us to perform those duties with hearts of love and lives of holiness.

For your journal...

1. The Lord promised to guide his people. Find some other Scriptures in which God promises guidance. List some ways in which God has guided you.

2. Write down some ways in which you can be a public blessing.

3. Can you identify conditions in churches today that make them like ruins? What can you do to bring renewal and restoration?

4. Look again at the duties God assigned his people in this passage (vv. 6-10). Are you fulfilling these duties? In what area, or areas, do you need to improve?

Isaiah 59:15-17

*Then the L*ORD *saw it, and it displeased him*
That there was no justice.
He saw that there was no man,
And wondered that there was no intercessor;
Therefore his own arm brought salvation for him;
And his own righteousness, it sustained him.
For he put on righteousness as a breastplate,
And a helmet of salvation on his head;
He put on the garments of vengeance for clothing,
And was clad with zeal as a cloak.

Day 20
What God saw; what God did

- ◆ *Begin by reading Isaiah 59*
- ◆ *Pray about what you have read*
- ◆ *Make notes on what you think God is teaching you*
- ◆ *Read the following chapter*
- ◆ *Answer the questions in the section 'For your journal'*

Isaiah 59:15-17

The prophet Isaiah lived in terrible times. A good portion of his life and ministry were spent during the evil reign of Judah's worst king. Here the prophet shares some of the disturbing details of life in Judah during Manasseh's reign.

Isaiah did this in order to help the captives in Babylon understand why they were there. It was not by accident. It was not due to some unfortunate and unexpected turn in political events. They were in captivity because of their sins. He also wanted to show them that they must avoid sinful living in the future if they were to enjoy the blessings of God.

We can go yet further and say that Isaiah did this in order to keep alive their faith in the coming Messiah. He talked at length about the reality of human sin so that he could point his readers to the only one who can deal with that dark and dreadful reality: to the Lord Jesus Christ. The terrible tyranny of sin can only be met by the amazing grace of God.

We join Isaiah, then, as he looks at his own evil time and as he rejoices in the sufficiency of God's grace. Isaiah presents these truths in terms of what the Lord saw and what the Lord did.

What the Lord saw (vv. 15-16)

'It'

Isaiah tells us that the Lord saw two things. First, we are told the Lord saw 'it' (v. 15). What is this 'it'? It is laid out for us in the first fifteen verses of this chapter. In short, the Lord saw a society that was filled with violence (v. 3), theft (v. 3), lying (v. 3), all manner of evil speaking (v. 3), and injustice (vv. 4, 9, 11, 14).

It was a society in which people had absolutely no regard or respect for the good and virtuous. It was a time in which,

> ...he who departs from evil
>   makes himself a prey
>
> (v. 15).

Imagine it! Those who tried to both be and do good found themselves preyed upon and victimized by others. Do we not see this very thing today? Do not those who try to do the right thing often find themselves more vilified than those who do wrong? Many churches who have tried to carry out the biblical teachings on church discipline could testify to this!

So the 'it' the Lord saw was the evil of Isaiah's day in raw and undiluted form.

'No intercessor'

The second thing the Lord saw was that 'there was no man … no intercessor' (v. 16). The Lord saw all the sin of Judah, and he also saw that there was absolutely no one who could do anything about that sin.

Isaiah tells us that the Lord 'wondered' over this. We would say he was amazed by it. We should not take this to mean that God was amazed in the sense of being taken by surprise. God cannot be surprised. Isaiah is here simply speaking of God in human terms to help us understand, and to emphasize for us the complete inability of sinners to help themselves.

The description that Isaiah gave of his own day applies equally to us. As the Lord looks upon us, he sees the very same things — sinfulness and total inability to extricate ourselves from sin. This is, of course, unpopular teaching, and there is certainly no shortage of objectors. When they hear what Scripture says about God seeing these things, they are eager to respond by talking about what they can and cannot see. These objectors hear about the reality of human sin and say, 'You preachers are always talking about sin, but I cannot see that man is so terrible.' They hear about the inability of man to save himself and say, 'It seems to me if a man does this or that, God will accept him.'

In raising these objections they essentially elevate themselves to God's level and suggest that their seeing is as good as his. And they fail to take into account that man cannot see the complete reality of his sin because he looks at himself with the eye of sin.

The supreme tragedy of those who fail to see the fact of human sin is that they cut themselves off from the cure for it. That cure is now presented to us by the prophet Isaiah.

What the Lord did (vv. 16-17)

How very thankful we should be that this passage does not end on a note of unrelieved gloom! Thank God that there is a 'therefore' here (v. 16). When the Lord saw that there was no other way by which sinful people could be delivered from their sins, he himself stepped in to provide deliverance. When he saw that sinners could not save themselves, he provided for them a way of salvation. When all was helpless and hopeless, the Lord stepped in.

What a breathtaking description Isaiah gives us of the Lord's work of salvation! It is the description of a mighty warrior.

His arm

The prophet first says of the Lord, 'His own arm brought salvation for him' (v. 16). Albert Barnes says, 'The idea is, that salvation was to be traced to God alone. It did not originate with man, and it was not accomplished by his agency or help.'[1]

His righteousness

Isaiah then says of the Lord, 'His own righteousness, it sustained him' (v. 16). Barnes interprets this phrase as follows: 'Sustained by the consciousness that he was doing right, he went forward against all opposition, and executed his plan.'[2]

His breastplate

The picture of the Lord as a warrior becomes even clearer with the next phrase: 'He put on righteousness as a breastplate' (v. 17). The breastplate was designed to protect the chest area. When the Lord Jesus Christ came to this earth to do the work of salvation, he was tempted by Satan; but he, the Lord Jesus, would not sin because he was covered in righteousness.

His helmet

Isaiah also says the Lord put on 'a helmet of salvation on his head' (v. 17). We can say that the Lord Jesus came to this earth and went about his ministry with the work of salvation constantly on his mind. He never lost sight of why he had come. When Satan sought to divert the Lord Jesus from this work, our Lord's helmet of salvation protected him.

His garments

The prophet further says the Lord 'put on the garments of vengeance' (v. 17). This means the Lord Jesus came to take vengeance on his foes. Yes, there are fierce and fearsome foes who have arrayed themselves against God and his plans. The evil one, Satan, is the greatest of these foes, but he is not alone. He heads up and presides over a kingdom of evil beings that are vehemently opposed to God (Eph. 6:12).

Satan succeeded in bringing sin into this world and sin has brought terrible heartache and havoc. The Lord God is not ambivalent about sin and all the harm it has done. He is angry about sin and angry at Satan, and his redeeming work was designed as an act of just vengeance against Satan (Col. 2:15).

His zeal

Finally, Isaiah says the Lord 'was clad with zeal as a cloak'
(v. 17). This means the Lord did not go reluctantly about the
work of salvation. He did it with zeal, that is, wholeheartedly
and fervently.

That zeal took him all the way to a Roman cross outside
Jerusalem where he stood in the place of sinners and received
the wrath of God that was due to them. We know what it is to
have faltering and flagging zeal. We are zealous for a while
only to give way to half-heartedness. We should rejoice that
our Lord did not go about the work of salvation in the same
fashion as we go about the work of serving him. We are saved
because of his unfailing zeal on our behalf.

It is again interesting that all the phrases used by the prophet
to describe the Lord undertaking the great work of salvation
are in the past tense. How could Isaiah, centuries before the
Lord Jesus Christ came, speak of this work as having already
been accomplished? The answer is that God was so completely
devoted to this work and so very capable of performing it that
Isaiah could speak of it as already having taken place.

The words of Isaiah must have provided tremendous comfort for the captives in Babylon. They knew their captivity
was due to their sinfulness. But as they read Isaiah's words
they had to realize that their sin, great as it was, was not greater
than God's grace.

> *My sin — oh, the bliss of this glorious tho't:*
> *My sin not in part, but the whole*
> *Is nail'd to the cross and I bear it no more,*
> *Praise the Lord, praise the Lord, O my soul.*
>
> Horatio G. Spafford, 'It is well with my soul'

For your journal...

1. The 'it' which the Lord saw was a society filled with evil. What do you think the Lord sees as he looks upon society today? Does this move you to pray more fervently?

2. The description of the Lord's armour in this passage makes us think of Paul's description of the Christian's armour in Ephesians 6:14-17. Does this show us that we are to be like our Lord? Write down the specific parts of the armour mentioned by Paul. What does each part mean? Are you utilizing each part?

Isaiah 60:1-3, 19-20

Arise, shine;
For your light has come!
And the glory of the LORD is risen upon you.
For behold, the darkness shall cover the earth,
And deep darkness the people;
But the LORD will arise over you,
And his glory will be seen upon you.
The Gentiles shall come to your light,
And kings to the brightness of your rising.

…

'The sun shall no longer be your light by day,
Nor for brightness shall the moon give light to you;
But the LORD will be to you an everlasting light,
And your God your glory.
Your sun shall no longer go down,
Nor shall your moon withdraw itself;
For the LORD will be your everlasting light,
And the days of your mourning shall be ended.'

Day 21
A new day and an endless day

- *Begin by reading Isaiah 60*
- *Pray about what you have read*
- *Make notes on what you think God is teaching you*
- *Read the following chapter*
- *Answer the questions in the section 'For your journal'*

Isaiah 60:1-3, 19-20

The prophecies of the Old Testament were given by God. They are, as is the case with every type of Scripture, unlike any other kind of literature. One of the unique features of these Old Testament prophecies is they sometimes move on two or three levels at the same time. In other words, they can have a double or even triple fulfilment.

The verses before us present us with these higher levels of fulfilment. The first level of fulfilment was achieved when the captives for whom Isaiah wrote returned from Babylon and rebuilt their homeland. But the language of these prophecies makes it clear that this was only partial fulfilment. The higher levels, as we shall note, were achieved later.

The verses we are considering deal with two types of days. The first set (vv. 1-3) presents the dawning of a new day. The second set (vv. 19-20) presents an endless day.

The new day: the day of salvation (vv. 1-3)

In these verses, Isaiah speaks of the dawning of a new day. The people who returned to Judah from their captivity in Babylon had no trouble relating this picture to their own experience. It was indeed a new day and a whole new world for them.

The people of Judah surely felt like they were living in deep darkness while they were living in Babylon. Furthermore, they probably wondered from time to time if the Lord had completely hidden himself from them. How different things were when they returned to their land! Their darkness gave way to light, and they could see the glory of the Lord all about them.

This dawning of a new day, this experience of the glory of the Lord, was something that made them quite distinct from the other nations. Those nations were still in darkness (v. 2), but the people of God were enjoying his light. We might think this distinctiveness would be resented by the other nations, but Isaiah says it would prove to be attractive. The nations would see the glory of God shining out of his people and would come to seek the light (vv. 2-3).

All of this is, of course, a perfect picture of salvation through Christ. His coming was like a mighty burst of light in a world of darkness. The brightness of his coming did indeed attract the Gentiles and even great kings.

This prophecy can also be applied to the salvation of each Christian. Like the Jews of Isaiah's day, we were living in deep darkness, the darkness of sin and condemnation, but the light of God has shined upon us through Christ and now we are living in a bright, new day (see 2 Cor. 4:4).

Those who do not know Christ are still in the deep darkness of sin, and we have the responsibility of rising and shining (v. 1) for Christ so that others will come to the light.

The endless day: the eternal day (vv. 19-20)

These verses bring us to the level of triple fulfilment. The first level again has to do with the return of the captives to their homeland. We must keep in mind that Isaiah is here using highly poetic and figurative language to describe the incredible exhilaration and joy this return would bring to the people. Their joy would be so great that it would make them feel as if they could never be unhappy again, as if their sun would 'no longer go down' (v. 20).

We find a second level of fulfilment in the period after Christ's first coming, the period of the church. Albert Barnes explains: 'The language here is exceedingly beautiful, and the idea is plain. It is designed to foretell the great glory which would exist in the church under the Messiah; a glory compared with which all that is furnished by the sun, moon and stars, would be as nothing.'[1]

To find the third and primary fulfilment of Isaiah's words, we have to look past the return of the captives, past the church, and into heaven itself. There can be no doubt at all about this because the apostle John's description of heaven in Revelation 21 relies heavily on these verses in Isaiah. For this reason, Derek Thomas is right to say, 'Ultimately, what we have here is a description of the glory of heaven itself. The prophet has "heaven in his eye".'[2]

While some argue that the Old Testament saints knew little or nothing at all about eternal glory in heaven, the author of the book of Hebrews does not hesitate to say, 'These all died in faith, not having received the promises, but having seen them afar off were assured of them, embraced them and confessed that they were strangers and pilgrims on the earth... But now they desire a better, that is, a heavenly country. Therefore God is not ashamed to be called their God, for he has prepared a city for them' (Heb. 11:13, 16).

What, then, does this passage in Isaiah tell us about the heaven, the new Jerusalem, that awaits the children of God? We focus on three features of that incredibly glorious place.

Heaven will be a happy place

Isaiah sets this before us by using the words 'joy' (v. 15) and 'peace' (v. 17) and by saying, 'the days of your mourning shall be ended' (v. 20). We know how happiness in this life is never complete and never lasting. We are happy for a while only to find our happiness diminished by some trial or sorrow. Even our happiest moments are tempered by the awareness of keen suffering and heartache all around us.

But our happiness in heaven will be undiluted and unending. Heaven will be a happy place because it will be a place of righteousness. Isaiah says, 'Also your people shall all be righteous' (v. 21). Sin is the cause of all our heartaches and sorrows, but sin will have no place in heaven. The apostle John says of it, 'And God will wipe away every tear from their eyes; there shall be no more death, nor sorrow, nor crying. There shall be no more pain, for the former things have passed away' (Rev. 21:4).

Heaven will be a place of praise

Isaiah puts it in these words:

> 'But you shall call ... your gates Praise'
>
> (v. 18).

And what will be the reason for this praise? Isaiah leaves no doubt about this.
He says:

> 'But you shall call your walls Salvation...'
>
> (v. 18).

The residents of heaven will be occupied with praise for the salvation that delivered them from eternal ruin and secured their glorious eternal home.
That inevitably brings us to another feature of heaven.

Heaven will be a God-centred and a Christ-centred place

Isaiah says,

> 'The sun shall no longer be your light by day,
> Nor for brightness shall the moon give light to you;
> But the LORD will be to you an everlasting light,
> And your God your glory.
> Your sun shall no longer go down,
> Nor shall your moon withdraw itself;
> For the LORD will be your everlasting light...'
>
> (vv. 19-20).

This is inevitably the case. If the residents of heaven are occupied with praise for salvation, they must be occupied with
the God who provided salvation. John tells us that the saints
of heaven will offer praise to Jesus Christ, the Lamb of God,
along these lines:

> 'You are worthy to take the scroll,
> And to open its seals;
> For you were slain,
> And have redeemed us to God by your blood
> Out of every tribe and tongue and people and nation...'
>
> (Rev. 5:9).

*But now at last, in the scene depicted in Revelation 5, the tides
of time have broken on the shore of eternity, and the people of
God enjoy the fruits of what that cross was all about. And, overwhelmed by it all, they break out into this song. This is the song
of the satisfied! They look upon God the Father who planned,
they look upon God the Son who executed, they look upon God
the Spirit who applied, and the testimony of their united hearts
is: 'He has done all things well.'*

Roger Ellsworth, Journey to the Cross[3]

Those who object to pastors and churches trying to be Christ-
centred in this world will not fit in heaven and, therefore,
have good reason to believe they will not be there.

This is a day in which multitudes casually assume that all
will be in heaven except perhaps the most villainous and vile.
They see heaven as being packed to the walls, while hell will
be sparsely populated with only the most vile and wicked. But
the Bible makes it clear that heaven will be populated only by

those who have repented of their sins and received the redeeming work of the Lord Jesus Christ (John 3:16, 36; 1 John 5:12).

The most important business in all of life, then, is making sure that we have Christ as our Lord and Saviour.

For your journal...

1. Recall that time when you came to faith in Christ. Did that feel to you like the dawning of a new day? Why?

2. Read Revelation 21 and 22. What parts of this description of eternity do you find most encouraging and meaningful?

Isaiah 61:10-11

I will greatly rejoice in the Lord,
My soul shall be joyful in my God;
For he has clothed me with the garments of salvation,
He has covered me with the robe of righteousness,
As a bridegroom decks himself with ornaments,
And as a bride adorns herself with her jewels.
For as the earth brings forth its bud,
As the garden causes the things that are sown in it to
*   spring forth,*
So the Lord God will cause righteousness and praise to
*   spring forth before all the nations.*

Day 22
Life's supreme blessing

- *Begin by reading Isaiah 61*
- *Pray about what you have read*
- *Make notes on what you think God is teaching you*
- *Read the following chapter*
- *Answer the questions in the section 'For your journal'*

Isaiah 61:10-11

The prophecy of Isaiah consists of sixty-six chapters. Its last twenty-seven chapters may be considered to be a book within a book. These chapters, which are bound together by the theme of comfort, can be called 'God's Book of Comfort'.

We have not been going through these chapters in a systematic or exhaustive way. We have rather lifted out of each chapter a 'nugget' of comfort. As we have worked our way through, we have frequently reminded ourselves of the original readers of these chapters. They were people who sorely needed comfort. They had seen their nation of Judah completely destroyed and had themselves been deported to Babylon.

Being enabled by the Spirit of God to see what these people would be going through, Isaiah wrote these chapters of comfort. We can be sure that the captives in Babylon found much consolation from reading them.

We come now to a particularly delightful nugget of comfort. The prophet here serves as a mouthpiece for the people of God in captivity and also for the people of God in every generation. His purpose in doing so was to remind them of life's supreme blessing. Yes, they had lost much and they were far away from home. But in the midst of it all, they could still say:

> I will greatly rejoice in the LORD,
> My soul shall be joyful in my God;
> For he has clothed me with the garments of salvation,
> He has covered me with the robe of righteousness,
> As a bridegroom decks himself with ornaments,
> And as a bride adorns herself with her jewels
>
> (v. 10).

Much of our happiness in life hinges on making the deliberate choice to look at our blessings even while we are in the midst of trying circumstances. And there is no greater blessing for us to gaze upon than the one reflected in this verse. Every child of God, no matter how severe his difficulties, can claim the glorious words of this verse for himself. And as he does so, he will find increased strength for bearing the difficulties.

What is life's supreme blessing? It is to be clothed with 'the garments of salvation' or 'the robe of righteousness'. This verse urges us to note four things about this clothing.

It is provided by God

The prophet writes: 'He has clothed me … he has covered me…' We cannot appreciate this if we do not understand that God demands something of us that we cannot possibly provide. What is it that God demands? It is that we have one hundred per cent perfection or he will not allow us to enter into heaven. He demands that we be as holy as he is.

There is no way that we can meet this demand. We cannot offer God the righteousness he requires. No matter how many good deeds we may do, we fall short. Any righteousness we suppose we possess is as filthy rags in the sight of God (Isa. 64:6). If we are to meet God's demand for righteousness, we must have what Martin Luther called an 'alien righteousness', that is, one that comes to us from the outside.

Is there any hope for us? There is! It is right there in the words of Isaiah: 'He has clothed me with the garments of salvation.' God has provided for sinners the very righteousness that he demands. He did so in and through his Son, the Lord Jesus Christ. I have not lived the righteous life that God demands, and you haven't either. But the Lord Jesus Christ has. He lived in perfect obedience to God's law. He did not break it in thought, word or deed.

The righteousness that Jesus provided by his life is imputed by God to sinners. That means he counts it as theirs. It is not theirs, but it is put to their account by God himself. The believing sinner is acceptable to God, then, because when God looks upon that sinner, he sees the righteousness of Jesus Christ.

That brings us to a second aspect of the clothing the prophet Isaiah rejoiced over.

It is provided for individuals

The prophet says:

> I will greatly rejoice in the LORD,
> My soul shall be joyful in my God;
> For he has clothed me with the garments of salvation.

We may wonder why Isaiah chose to use 'I', 'my' and 'me' when he was addressing all the captives in Babylon. Perhaps the explanation is that he wanted them to understand that the blessing of salvation comes to us on an individual basis.

How often the people of Israel misunderstood this! They frequently fell into the trap of thinking they were right with God simply because of their nationality, because they were born Jews. But being a Jew did not make anyone a child of God! Salvation belonged only to Jews of faith. It was not having the *genes* of Abraham, but having the *faith* of Abraham that made a true child of Abraham (Gal. 3:7-9, 29).

Many today have fallen into the same trap. They think they are saved because they are part of a church or because they are part of a 'Christian' nation. But salvation is an individual matter. We are not saved by saying, 'God has covered my church' or 'God has covered my nation.' We are saved only if we can truthfully say, 'God has covered me.'

Religion is a matter of personal pronouns. It is a matter of saying to God, 'my God', and hearing him say in return, 'my child'. The individual nature of salvation was powerfully underscored by the Lord Jesus Christ in his parable of the wedding garment (Matt. 22:1-14). The king had invited many to the wedding feast for his son, and the wedding hall was filled with guests. But the king insisted that each individual be clothed in the wedding garment that he, the king, had provided.

There was one man there who did not think it necessary to clothe himself in the required garment. When an attendant offered it to him, he may very well have brushed himself down a little and said, 'My own garment is good enough.' He may even have assured himself that he would not be noticed among so many guests. But he *was* noticed. The king came into the wedding hall, immediately spotted the man, walked right up to him and said, 'Friend, how did you come in here without a wedding garment?' (Matt. 22:12).

As the master of that wedding feast dealt personally with that man, we may be sure that the Lord will deal personally with each of us on this matter of salvation.

Let us now turn to a third noteworthy feature of the clothing of salvation.

It is to be received as a gift

Note again the prophet's words: '...God ... has clothed me'. He does not say that he has clothed himself in the garments of salvation; it was the Lord who clothed him. *The Lord* had provided the garments of salvation. *The Lord* had stripped off the prophet's filthy rags. *The Lord* had put the garments of salvation on the prophet. Those who are truly saved understand that their salvation is not a matter of their own doing. It is a matter of God's grace.

That brings us to a final feature of the clothing of salvation.

It is entirely sufficient for us

John Gill finds significance in the word 'garments'. He concludes that the plural suggests 'the fulness and completeness
of this salvation, from all sin, from wrath, hell, and damna-
tion, and from every enemy...'[1]

What a blessed joy it is to ponder this! The salvation provided by the Lord covers everything. Clothed in such garments,
no one has to fear the devil or anyone else pointing out any
flaw or deficiency. The salvation provided by Christ on the
cross covers it all.

Calvary covers it all,
My past with its sin and stain;
My guilt and despair
Jesus took on Him there,
And Calvary covers it all

  Mrs Walter G. Taylor, 'Calvary covers it all'

The devil is, of course, the accuser of the people of God. He
enjoys pointing at the children of God and saying, 'Under their
garments, they are filthy and vile.' But the Lord God looks
upon them and says, 'All I can see is the righteousness of my
Son, Jesus Christ.'

What a joy it is to have the garments of salvation! They
indeed constitute life's supreme blessing. If you do not have
them, the most urgent matter of business for you is to seek
them. Come to God in your sin and ask him to clothe you.

If you do have them, you should be rejoicing in them even
as the prophet did. Take his words as your own:

I will greatly rejoice in the LORD,
My soul shall be joyful in my God;
For he has clothed me with the garments of salvation.

Great salvation demands great praise. Away then with our faint praise!

For your journal...

1. What burdens and difficulties are you facing right now? Are you able to rejoice in God's salvation even while you are in the midst of difficulty?

2. What do you think about this statement: 'Great salvation demands great praise'? Would you characterize your praise as 'great'? What can you do to increase your praise?

Isaiah 62:4

You shall no longer be termed Forsaken,
Nor shall your land any more be termed Desolate;
But you shall be called Hephzibah, and your land Beulah;
For the LORD delights in you,
And your land shall be married.

Day 23
Hephzibah: God's delight in his people

- ♦ *Begin by reading Isaiah 62*
- ♦ *Pray about what you have read*
- ♦ *Make notes on what you think God is teaching you*
- ♦ *Read the following chapter*
- ♦ *Answer the questions in the section 'For your journal'*

Isaiah 62:4

It is very difficult to remain balanced in our handling of Scripture. Without realizing what we are doing, we can easily fall into the trap of emphasizing one aspect of truth while ignoring another that is equally valid.

We pastors have to fight constantly against such a tendency. It is very easy for us to see what the church can and should be, and then see our people falling short of the ideal. With this in mind, we find ourselves constantly telling our people about their deficiencies and urging them to be, and to do, better.

This is, of course, a legitimate message. The Bible abounds with texts that provide for this type of preaching. But the danger is that in preaching in this way, we will give our people the impression that God is always angry with them and that they are never in any way pleasing to him.

We have in our text the other side of the coin. Here God uses the prophet Isaiah to tell his people that he, God, delights in his people; that he takes pleasure in them.

Have you thought recently about God having pleasure? Many of us have a picture of God that has no room for pleasure at all. We see him as a rather miserable being who only enjoys depriving his creatures of pleasure and making them as unhappy as he is himself. But this text — and several others as well — gives us a completely different picture. God has his pleasures, and one of his pleasures is his people. This is not to say that God does not care about the sins of his people. The captives in Babylon could have given eloquent testimony to how seriously God views sin. Their captivity was due to their failure to live as God had commanded, and God's resultant punishment upon them.

Yet the fact that a parent finds it necessary to punish a child does not mean that he does not love or delight in that child. It proves just the opposite. He disciplines the child because he loves him so very much and desires the best for him.

We know those captives in Babylon keenly felt the weight of their sin. They knew that God had judged them and they knew they deserved every ounce of his judgement. Perhaps they felt that God was so angry with them that he would never again have anything to do with them.

What a comfort it was to those captives to read the words of our text! God still found delight in them as his people. He would restore them to their land (v. 4) and cause the Gentiles and their kings to see their glory (v. 2).

Brother or sister in Christ, you are no doubt conscious of great failure. You can name a thousand things that you should have done for the Lord and failed to do. You can name another thousand things that you should not have done. And the devil is now sitting on your shoulder and whispering in your ear. He tells you that your failures are so great that God could not possibly love you, that God is sitting in heaven in a boiling rage and looking for the first opportunity to drop the hammer on you.

Will you try to crawl into the words of this text and find comfort and consolation? Will you listen to the testimony of God himself that he finds delight in his people? The Lord is not under any illusions about you. He knows your failings. He can even name failures of which you are not aware, and he does not take them lightly. But he still delights in you as his child.

What is there about his people that brings God pleasure and delight?

Their clothing

First, we can say God delights in his people because they are clothed in the righteousness of Christ. It is not accidental that our text follows so closely the final verses of chapter 61. There we found the prophet rejoicing in the robe of righteousness, which has been provided by Christ and imputed by God to his people.

God takes pleasure in his Son (Matt. 17:5). Anyone clothed in the righteousness of his Son, then, has to bring pleasure to God.

Their prayers

In the second place, the Lord takes pleasure in the prayers of his people. The author of Proverbs writes:

> The sacrifice of the wicked is an abomination to the LORD,
> But the prayer of the upright is his delight
>
> (Prov. 15:8).

We do not take pleasure in our own prayers. They sound so very weak and feeble, as if they are nothing more than the idle babbling of a babe. But as the parent finds pleasure in the babbling of his child, so the Lord finds pleasure in the prayers of his people.

We find it very difficult to pray. We cannot seem to find the time for it, and we do not seem to find much pleasure in it. How helpful it would be for us to remember that the God who made us and saved us finds pleasure in our prayers!

Their reverence

Thirdly, God finds delight in the reverence his people have for him. Psalm 147:11 says of God:

> The LORD takes pleasure in those who fear him...

No Christian holds an adequate measure of reverence for God, but every child of God fears him. What is it to fear the Lord? It is to stand in awe of his person and to dread his displeasure.

Their hope

Fourthly, God takes pleasure in the hope of his people. Psalm 147:11 also says,

> The LORD takes pleasure...
> In those who hope in his mercy.

To hope in the mercy of God is to live with anticipation of receiving the things that God has prepared for us.

We must say again that no child of God has hope to the extent that he should, but it is present in every child of God. To the degree that God sees that hope in us, he rejoices in us.

Their obedience

We can also say the Lord takes pleasure in the obedience of his people. The prophet Samuel powerfully made this point to King Saul:

> 'Has the LORD as great delight in burnt offerings and sacrifices,
> As in obeying the voice of the LORD?'
> (1 Sam. 15:22).

Just as the disobedience of his people displeases the Lord, so each act of obedience brings him pleasure. No child of God perfectly obeys, but each child of God agrees that the commandments of God are good and right, seeks to live according to those commandments, feels grief and pain when he fails to obey and eventually comes to repentance.

Their way

In the next place, we can say the Lord delights in the way of his people. The psalmist David wrote:

> The steps of a good man are ordered by the LORD,
> And he delights in his way
>
> (Ps. 37:23).

God's people have a way. That way takes them from their sin and condemnation to forgiveness of sins and sanctification. It takes them through many 'dangers, toils and snares', and finally brings them home to heaven. God is the one who has established this way for his people, and, as he sees each one travelling this way, he finds pleasure and delight.

Their homecoming

Finally, we can say God takes delight in the expectation of receiving his people unto himself. The author of Hebrews says that the Lord Jesus Christ endured the cross 'for the joy that was set before him' (Heb. 12:2).

The prophet Isaiah himself was enabled to look down the corridor of time and see the Lord Jesus dying on the cross. As he did so, the prophet wrote of Christ:

> He shall see the labour of his soul, and be satisfied
>
> (Isa. 53:11).

Both verses tell us that the Lord Jesus looked beyond the cross to what it was intended to achieve, that is, the gathering of the people of God into heaven. As Jesus saw this, he found joy and satisfaction. Because Christ's death was ordained by God, the joy and satisfaction Christ had was shared by his Father.

We who have received that redeeming death also look forward to that time, and we, too, feel joy and satisfaction. We are not a perfect people, and we often feel as if the Lord must be thoroughly disgusted with us. But when redemption's work is finally done and we are gathered around the throne, we will have undeniable proof of the delight that God takes in his people. And we will rejoice in him as he rejoices in us.

> *She is led out to the King. This is the moment of marriage. He is to take her to himself for the procession back to the palace. Publicly, before all the astounded world of angels and nations the Christ gallantly receives the bride. Now it is one thing for a sinner to receive Jesus as his Lord. It is infinitely more marvellous to behold the Lord receive the transformed sinner as his beloved bride.*
>
> Walter Chantry, Praises for the King of Kings[1]

For your journal...

1. Did you come to this chapter with the feeling that God is never pleased with you? How has this chapter helped you?

2. How do you feel about your prayer life? Does the knowledge that God delights in your prayers encourage you to be more faithful in this area?

Isaiah 63:7-10

I will mention the lovingkindnesses of the Lᴏʀᴅ
And the praises of the Lᴏʀᴅ,
According to all that the Lᴏʀᴅ has bestowed on us,
And the great goodness toward the house of Israel,
Which he has bestowed on them according to his mercies,
According to the multitude of his lovingkindnesses.
For he said, 'Surely they are my people,
Children who will not lie.'
So he became their Saviour.
In all their affliction he was afflicted,
And the Angel of his Presence saved them;
In his love and in his pity he redeemed them;
And he bore them and carried them
All the days of old.
But they rebelled and grieved his Holy Spirit;
So he turned himself against them as an enemy,
And he fought against them.

Day 24
What to mention in times of trouble

- ◆ Begin by reading Isaiah 63
- ◆ Pray about what you have read
- ◆ Make notes on what you think God is teaching you
- ◆ Read the following chapter
- ◆ Answer the questions in the section 'For your journal'

Isaiah 63:7-10

Christians and non-Christians often mention the same things. The weather, sports, politics and family matters are prominent among our common discussions. But the people of God are known for a special mentioning. They mention the Lord (Isa. 62:6; Ps. 71:16). The Lord is a natural part of his people's conversations. They look at life through a special grid. They think of it in terms of the Lord and his purposes. They interpret it on the basis of the Lord and his teachings.

Unbelievers often mention the Lord in a profane way, but believers treat the Lord's name with reverence and mention it with respect.

The prophet Isaiah wrote the words of our text, as we have been noting throughout, for his people who would be taken into captivity by the Babylonians. Isaiah was enabled by the Spirit of God to look down the corridor of time and see with clarity what would befall his people. He wrote the last twenty-seven chapters of this prophecy to provide comfort and encouragement for those captives.

Those people would desperately need such comfort. They would be in dire straits indeed. Their captivity would mean that they would have lost their homes, their temple and their nation. It would mean being in a land which constantly pressured them to abandon their faith. These captives would know the meaning of trouble.

In this passage Isaiah gives them guidance for handling such trouble. They are to remember to mention the Lord while in their captivity. As the people of God, they were known for mentioning the Lord. They must not forget to mention him in their trouble.

This has tremendous relevance for those of us who belong to the Lord. We are also known for talking about him. We mention him in worship. We mention him in prayer. We mention him in our conversations. But do we remember to mention God in our troubles?

Many Christians fail here. They are happy to mention God when things are going well, but they get upset with God when their circumstances turn sour. If they mention him in their difficulty it is only to complain that he has mistreated them.

What should we who know the Lord mention about him in our times of trial? Isaiah gives us the answer to this question. He sums it all up in these words: 'I will mention the lovingkindnesses of the LORD...' (v. 7).

The lovingkindness of the Lord

What is the lovingkindness of the Lord? It is kindness that has love in it. It is the disposition of God to treat his people kindly because of the immense love he has for them. It is his disposition to treat his people with affectionate tenderness.

Its staggering nature

The prophet's treatment of this subject enables us to note two aspects.

First, there is the staggering nature of God's lovingkindness. Isaiah seems to no sooner mention this to his people than he realizes he is in over his head. It is as if he is struggling to convey this adequately. Notice that he uses the plural 'lovingkindnesses'. God has expressed his lovingkindness, not just in one way, but in many. Isaiah emphasizes this by referring to 'the multitude' of God's lovingkindnesses (v. 7). He also uses the phrase 'all that the LORD has bestowed on us' (v. 7). The impression is that God has done a great deal for his people. He proceeds to write of 'the great goodness' of God. God's goodness is not tiny or minuscule. It is huge.

We who know the Lord acknowledge that he has been lovingly kind to us, but we are blind to the measure of this lovingkindness. We see only the tip of the iceberg. God is always and unfailingly kind to his people, every day and in every way. He is kind even when he appears not to be.

Its specific manifestations

Isaiah's words also compel us to note the specific manifestations of his lovingkindness. The prophet was not content merely to urge the people to remember the lovingkindnesses of the Lord, he also calls upon them to remember certain expressions of that lovingkindness.

Choosing. He first reminds them of God's choice of them. God had made them his people (v. 8). They were not God's people because they were in some way better or more deserving than others. They were his people because in grace he had set his heart upon them and decided to make them his.

God's people today can rejoice in this same aspect of God's lovingkindness, for we have also been chosen by the Lord (Eph. 1:3-4).

Saving. The prophet also reminds them of God's saving work on their behalf. Isaiah uses various phrases to drive this point home. He says God 'became their Saviour' (v. 8). He also writes:

> And the Angel of his Presence saved them;
> In his love and in his pity he redeemed them...
>
> (v. 9).

The prophet was probably referring to God saving or delivering their forefathers from bondage in Egypt. The 'Angel of his Presence', which occurs several times in the Old Testament, probably refers to a pre-incarnate appearance of the Lord Jesus Christ. That one specific act of deliverance was symbolic of a far greater act, that is, salvation from sins.

Salvation from sin is, of course, the single greatest expression of God's lovingkindness. Let there be no mistake here — that salvation is only through the redeeming work of the Lord Jesus Christ. He took our humanity, lived in perfect obedience to God and went to the cross where he endured the wrath of God against sinners.

What love we have here! God sending his own Son to save us!

> *This love appears altogether astonishing when we consider the* **greatness of the sacrifice** *it made. That God himself (infinite, eternal, and self-sufficient as he was) should bring himself down to a mortal form; that he who made the heavens should descend from among the adoration of angels to assume the form of a servant and to receive the spittings of Roman soldiers; that he should exchange the quiet of eternal repose for a laborious life — the abodes of inaccessible light for the degrading manger — the society of the Father and Spirit for that of illiterate fishermen — the heights of infinite bliss for the agonies of Gethsemane and Golgotha — and all to atone for abuses which he himself had received from men; fixes angels in astonishment and rivets their eyes to him who still bears the prints of the nails and the spear* (emphasis is his).
>
> Edward D. Griffin,
> The Life and Sermons of Edward D. Griffin[1]

Afflicting. Isaiah identifies yet another expression of God's lovingkindness for his people. It is one that may surprise us: it is God afflicting them.

The prophet puts God on a very human level to aid us in our understanding. He tells us that God had a certain expectation of his people, that is, that they would not 'lie' (v. 8). In other words, God expected his people to be true to him.

The fact that Isaiah was addressing himself to captives in Babylon tells us that God was disappointed in his expectations. His people 'rebelled and grieved his Holy Spirit' (v. 10). We must not take Isaiah's words to mean that God was surprised or taken off guard by this. God knows all things. Isaiah was only speaking of God in human terms.

Because his people rebelled against him, the Lord brought affliction upon them. We tend to regard affliction as God withdrawing his lovingkindness from us. It is exactly the opposite. It is because God loves his people that he chastises them, just as the parent who loves his child disciplines him.

Sharing. That brings us to a further manifestation of God's lovingkindness, that is, God sharing the affliction of his people. Isaiah says, 'In all their affliction he was afflicted' (v. 9).

God does not take delight in chastising his people. He afflicts them for their good, but he himself feels the pain of their affliction and suffers with them.

Isaiah then adds another expression of God's lovingkindness, namely, his bearing and carrying them (v. 9). This probably refers to God patiently sustaining his people through the whole period from their deliverance from Egypt to Isaiah's own time. Matthew Henry writes of God: '...he supported them when they were burdened, and ready to sink, he bore them up; in the wars they made upon the nations he stood by them and bore them out; though they were peevish, he bore with them and suffered their manners... He carried them as the nursing father does the child, though they would have tired any arms but his; he carried them as the eagle her young upon her wings...'[2]

Isaiah had, then, no shortage of evidences for the lovingkindness of God. And everything he said about God's lovingkindnesses to Israel of old applies equally well to us.

Why did the prophet emphasize the lovingkindnesses of God? He had a very simple reason. It was to drive his people to this inexorable conclusion — if God had been so kind in the past, they could believe that he would be kind in the future. This confidence would then lead them to pray for the mercies of God (63:15 - 64:12).

We need this reminder of God's lovingkindnesses so that in the midst of our troubles we can believe that God still loves us and will continue to be kind to us.

For your journal...

1. Do you mention God's lovingkindnesses when you are facing trouble? Write down some ways in which God has been lovingly kind to you.

2. Have you thought of your troubles as expressions of God's lovingkindness? How do our problems manifest God's love for us?

Isaiah 64:1-4, 6, 9

Oh, that you would rend the heavens!
That you would come down!
That the mountains might shake at your presence —
As fire burns brushwood,
As fire causes water to boil —
To make your name known to your adversaries,
That the nations may tremble at your presence!
When you did awesome things for which we did not look,
You came down,
The mountains shook at your presence.
For since the beginning of the world
Men have not heard nor perceived by the ear,
Nor has the eye seen any God besides you,
Who acts for the one who waits for him.
…
But we are all like an unclean thing,
And all our righteousnesses are like filthy rags;
We all fade as a leaf,
And our iniquities, like the wind,
Have taken us away.
…
Do not be furious, O Lord,
Nor remember iniquity for ever…

Day 25
A prayer for revival

- ♦ Begin by reading Isaiah 64
- ♦ Pray about what you have read
- ♦ Make notes on what you think God is teaching you
- ♦ Read the following chapter
- ♦ Answer the questions in the section 'For your journal'

Isaiah 64:1-4, 6, 9

This chapter continues and concludes the prayer that the prophet began in the preceding chapter (63:15). This prayer was given to the prophet Isaiah many years before the captivity began. It would become the prayer of the captives themselves as they reflected on the reasons for their exile and yearned for it to end. It must have been a prized source of comfort and encouragement to them. We will look at two reasons why this was so.

God wanted them to pray

This suggests two very important truths.

God did not regard their failure as final

We can well imagine how very easy it would have been for them to feel as if God wanted nothing more to do with them. But the fact that they had this prayer assured them that this was not the case. It showed that God wanted to hear from them. He had not utterly cast them off and disowned them. God would not have given it if he had not intended his people to use it, or if its use would be fruitless.

The captivity did not mean that God was washing his hands of his people; it was rather God washing his people. In other words, God did not use the captivity to disown his people but rather, to cleanse them. He is truly a God with supreme patience.

Are you mindful that you have failed God? Do you sometimes feel that your failures are so many and so great that God has written you off? You can find consolation in Isaiah's prayer. It tells you that God is not finished with you; he wants to hear from you.

Then there is the second truth suggested by the captives' possession of this prayer.

The value God places on prayer

The way back to God always takes us through the gate of prayer. There can be no true revival without it. Spiritual renewal produces prayer as surely as sunshine and rain cause plants to grow.

That great theologian of revival, Jonathan Edwards, offered this observation about God's dealings with his people: 'When he is about to bestow some great blessing on his church, it is often his manner, in the first place, so to order things in his providence, as to show his church their great need of it, and to bring them into distress for want of it, and so put them upon crying earnestly to him for it.'[1]

Many Scriptures connect revival and prayer. The best known of these is undoubtedly 2 Chronicles 7:14, which reports the Lord saying, '...if my people who are called by my name will humble themselves, and pray and seek my face, and turn from their wicked ways, then I will hear from heaven, and will forgive their sin and heal their land'.

The psalmist Asaph prayed for revival in this way:

Restore us, O God of hosts;
Cause your face to shine,
And we shall be saved!

(Ps. 80:7).

He also prays:

Revive us, and we will call upon your name

(v. 18).

Another psalmist prayed in this way:

Will you not revive us again,
That your people may rejoice in you?

(Ps. 85:6).

Scripture's unrelenting emphasis on prayer led Jonathan Edwards to say: 'There is no way that Christians in a private capacity can do so much to promote the work of God and advance the kingdom of Christ, as by prayer ... if they have much of the spirit of grace and supplication, in this way they may have power with him who is infinite in power and has the government of the whole world. A poor man in his cottage may have a blessed influence all over the world.'[2]

The great question, then, is this: are we praying for a mighty moving of God in our midst? Are we pleading with him for it? If we want God to visit with us and do his extraordinary work of revival, we must pray earnestly. It is as simple as that.

It should not escape our notice that Isaiah included the word 'wait' in his prayer. He says the Lord 'acts for the one who waits for him' (v. 4). The word translated 'wait' has an affinity with a Hebrew word that means 'entrench'. We might say, therefore, that to wait on God means to dig in with determination. It means to shut ourselves up unto God with a singleness of mind and purpose.

Do we have here the reason why we are seeing so very little of true revival? I think we do. As long as we are content to pay mere lip service to revival, it will not come. We must wait. We must pursue it with dogged determination. May God create within us even now that spirit of waiting.

> *But when we take hold of God it is as the boatman with his hook takes hold on the shore, as if he would pull the shore to him, but really it is to pull himself to the shore; so we pray, not to bring God to our mind, but to bring ourselves to his.*
>
> *Matthew Henry,* Matthew Henry's Commentary[3]

This side of eternity we will never understand how much God prizes prayer. The book of Revelation speaks of God keeping the prayers of his people in bowls (Rev. 5:8). What must prayer be to God if he keeps it in bowls?

The captives must also have found this prayer to be encouraging for another reason.

God told them what to ask

Anyone who knows anything about prayer easily identifies with the words of the apostle Paul: '...we do not know what we should pray for as we ought...' (Rom. 8:26). Every believer can say a hearty 'Amen!' to the request the disciples put to Jesus: 'Lord, teach us to pray...' (Luke 11:2).

As the captives in Babylon studied this prayer, they would immediately see two petitions that they should put before God diligently and persistently.

They were to ask God to demonstrate his power (vv. 1-4)

The nation of Israel had experienced astonishing things. She had seen God intervene on her behalf and show his strength. The most obvious example of this is, of course, the exodus from Egypt. But there was also that great victory over Amalek, the miraculous crossing of the Jordan, and the toppling of the walls of Jericho. If Isaiah had been asked to summarize the great acts of God in Israel's history, he might very well have said, 'God came down!'

The captives for whom Isaiah wrote his prayer would find themselves facing huge problems: securing their release from Babylon, returning to their homeland and rebuilding their individual lives and their nation.

To use the imagery of Isaiah's prayer, these problems would seem as big as a mountain and as tangled as brushwood. They would be equivalent to one seeking to make ice cold water boil without so much as a single match in his hand (vv. 1-2). In short, the problem of captivity was so great that it could only be solved by God doing what he had done in the past;

that is, by coming down from heaven and once again showing his zeal, his strength and his affection for his people. The good news was that the God who had so frequently solved insurmountable problems in the nation's history was ready and willing to do so again.

They were to ask God to forgive their sins (vv. 6-9)

They were to come before God saying:

> But we are all like an unclean thing,
> And all our righteousnesses are like filthy rags;
> We all fade as a leaf,
> And our iniquities, like the wind,
> Have taken us away
>
> (v. 6).

They were also to say:

> Do not be furious, O LORD,
> Nor remember iniquity for ever
>
> (v. 9).

These are words of confession, and we can be sure that God would not have given them words of confession if he were not willing to grant forgiveness to his people.

The Bible abounds with God's promises to freely grant forgiveness. Through the prophet Hosea, the Lord instructed the people of Israel:

> Take words with you,
> And return to the LORD.

Say to him,
'Take away all iniquity;
Receive us graciously,
For we will offer the sacrifices of our lips'

(Hosea 14:2).

God then indicated how he would respond:

'I will heal their backsliding,
I will love them freely,
For my anger has turned away from him'

(14:4).

The apostle John assured his readers that God was willing to forgive: 'If we confess our sins, he is faithful and just to forgive us our sins and to cleanse us from all unrighteousness' (1 John 1:9).

While the captives could come to God with the assurance that he would forgive, they still had to confess. It is interesting that the prayer God gave them does not blame the Babylonians for the captivity. It recognizes that the Babylonians were not the cause; they were only God's instrument. The real cause was the flagrant disobedience of God's people (64:5-7).

This also carries a powerful message for us. Nothing is more common in the church today than 'blaming the Babylonians'. In other words, we explain the loss of spiritual power and vitality in terms of the times in which we live and the circumstances which we face.

We might, for example, find ourselves thinking the people of God in former times experienced revival because they had more time for the things of God and had fewer pressures than we do. But this is nothing more than blaming the Babylonians, and there can be no true revival as long as we engage in it.

Revival comes to those who put the blame for their spiritual coldness and apathy where it belongs: on themselves and their failure to live according to God's laws.

For your journal...

1. Look up the words 'forgive' and 'forgiveness' in a concordance. Make a note of those verses that speak most pointedly to you. Make a list of things for which you need to ask God's forgiveness.

2. How important is prayer in your life? Write down some ways in which you can improve in this area.

Isaiah 65:17-19

'For behold, I create new heavens and a new earth;
And the former shall not be remembered or come to mind.
But be glad and rejoice for ever in what I create;
For behold, I create Jerusalem as a rejoicing,
And her people a joy.
I will rejoice in Jerusalem,
And joy in my people;
The voice of weeping shall no longer be heard in her,
Nor the voice of crying.'

Day 26
Good things to know about God

- *Begin by reading Isaiah 65*
- *Pray about what you have read*
- *Make notes on what you think God is teaching you*
- *Read the following chapter*
- *Answer the questions in the section 'For your journal'*

Isaiah 65:17-19

As we noticed in the last chapter, the prophecy of Isaiah includes a prayer that his readers would be praying during their captivity in Babylon (63:15 - 64:12). This would be a prayer of repentance and a prayer for spiritual renewal. It would be a plea for God to act on behalf of his people and release them from their captivity.

This prayer would include the following petition:

Do not be furious, O Lord,
Nor remember iniquity for ever

(64:9).

We must keep Isaiah's prayer in mind as we come to this sixty-fifth chapter of his prophecy. In particular, we must keep in mind the plea of the people for God not to keep his anger for ever.

We can well imagine how the captives might be inclined to think that the Lord would retain his anger towards them. They had sinned very grievously and had continued in their sins even though God sent prophet after prophet to call them to repentance.

As the captives reflected on the depth of their sin, they may have been inclined to believe that the Lord would never again have anything to do with them. Perhaps they thought that God had cancelled all his promises. There would never again be a nation of Israel. There would never again be a city of Jerusalem. There would never again be a temple. And maybe there would never be a Messiah.

The verses of chapter 65 must have been an immense comfort to the captives. It contains wonderful assurances that God would not be angry for ever but would give them a future that would be too glorious for words. It was a future that would seem too good to be true. But it would come true because God himself promised it.

This future would feature several things. The people would be restored to their land (vv. 9, 21). The land itself would be wonderfully productive (v. 10). The people would enjoy long lives (vv. 20, 22). This future would be so grand and glorious that the people would require new ways to describe it. It would be as if everything old had passed away and all things had become new, as if there were new heavens and a new earth (v. 17). It would feature circumstances so unusual and out of keeping with the ordinary that it would be as if the wolf and the lamb would feed together (v. 25).

As we read these descriptions, we are reminded again of that phenomenon which we have encountered previously, that

of multiple fulfilment. The return of the captives would constitute one level of fulfilment, but there would be even more
exact and blessed fulfilments in the future.

Let us look at this matter of the new heavens and the new
earth, for example. As noted, the experience of the returning
captives would be such that it would seem as if a new heaven
and a new earth had been created. But when he gave Isaiah
these words God had far more in mind than the return of the
captives from Babylon. The book of Revelation makes it clear
that there will actually be a new heaven, a new earth and a
new Jerusalem (Rev. 21:1-4).

We do well, then, to look beyond the meaning these verses
would have had for the returning captives to its higher fulfilment in eternity itself. We cannot look at these verses without
noticing that God himself is speaking in them. What glorious
truths God reveals about himself here!

He is a great and glorious God

We can see the greatness of God by looking up at the sky. In
one of his many psalms, David wrote:

> The heavens declare the glory of God;
> And the firmament shows his handiwork
>
> (Ps. 19:1).

We can see the greatness of God by looking at the earth as it is
now. The mighty ocean tides crashing on the shore, the ma-
jestic mountains, the stately trees, the wide variety of animals
and the beautifully delicate flowers all give eloquent testimony
to the wisdom and power of God.

If we can see the greatness of God in the heavens and on the earth as they are now, stained by the sinfulness of men, how much more will we be able to see the greatness of God in the new heavens and the new earth!

He is a redeeming God

What a marvellous truth we have here! How very miserable we would be if this were not the case! This brings us, of course, to the central truth of Scripture — paradise lost through sin, and regained through Christ.

Let's re-examine this theme for a moment. The Bible tells us that God created all things good. But Adam and Eve disobeyed God and introduced sin into the human race.

God did not have to redeem fallen sinners. He could have left us in our sins and would have been completely justified in doing so. But God would not do so. Before Adam and Eve ever sinned, God had a plan of redemption in place. That plan consisted of the second person of the Trinity, the Lord Jesus Christ, taking unto himself our humanity. In that humanity he would live in perfect obedience to God's laws and he would go to the cross and there receive the wrath of God in the place of his people.

The good news of the Bible is that all who rely completely on the redeeming work of the Lord Jesus Christ regain the paradise that was lost through sin. It is not mere coincidence that the Bible opens with access to the Tree of Life being denied, and closes with access to that same tree being granted. The word 'redemption' involves putting things back to where they were. The very fact that God promises to create new heavens and a new earth means God's plan of redemption will succeed. Even the earth itself, so brutalized by man's sin, will be restored to its original beauty and glory.

This ought to make us realize that the final state for believers will not have them floating on clouds and strumming harps. Our eternal state will be under the new heavens and on the new earth, as John so beautifully describes in Revelation 21 and 22.

There is yet another truth we can glean about God from what he says in our text about himself.

He is a happy God

If you have the notion that God is a miserable being who only enjoys making his creatures unhappy, you are completely wrong!

Look at what the Lord says:

'For behold, I create Jerusalem as a rejoicing,
And her people a joy'

(v. 18).

Now we know that the new Jerusalem, that heavenly city that God will place on the new earth, will bring joy to the hearts of his people. But that is not what the Lord is talking about in these words. He goes on to explain:

'I will rejoice in Jerusalem,
And joy in my people;
The voice of weeping shall no longer be heard in her,
Nor the voice of crying'

(v. 19).

God himself is going to experience unspeakable joy when the process of redemption is complete and all his people are finally home.

> *God himself rejoices in his people, as they are considered in Christ; so he did from all eternity, and so he does at the conversion of them; which is the day of their espousals, and when he manifests his love to them, and rejoices over them to do them good, and continues to do so; and he rejoices in the exercise of his own grace in them, and will do so throughout ... all eternity.*
> *John Gill,* Exposition of the Old & New Testaments[1]

The author of Hebrews indicates that the Lord Jesus was able to endure the extreme anguish of the cross because of 'the joy that was set before him' (Heb. 12:2). Many think that joy was nothing less than seeing the people for whom he died gathered together in the new Jerusalem.

We cannot begin to understand all the components in the joy of God. But we know that God will rejoice because his people will weep no more. The book of Revelation tells us that God himself will wipe every tear from the eyes of his people. And when God does this wiping away with his great celestial handkerchief, it will not be necessary for him to ever use that handkerchief again. Their weeping will be over for ever.

Now if God will receive in glory such delight in wiping away the tears of his people, can we not conclude that he is even now moved by our tears and touched by our suffering? And if God will be so very happy at the end of redemption's story, are we not entitled to conclude that he is happy even now as he works to move redemption to that glorious end?

I do not know what you are suffering these days. I do not know how heavy is your burden or how sharp your pain. But if you are a believer in Jesus Christ, there is comfort and consolation for you in resting on these truths: your God is a great God, a redeeming God and a happy God.

For your journal...

1. What has been your way of thinking about the believer's final state? Have you thought of it in terms of this earth being restored to the way it was created? Does this comfort you?

2. Have you ever thought of God as being happy? How does his happiness bring comfort to you?

Isaiah 66:10-13

'Rejoice with Jerusalem,
And be glad with her, all you who love her;
Rejoice for joy with her, all you who mourn for her;
That you may feed and be satisfied
With the consolation of her bosom,
That you may drink deeply and be delighted
With the abundance of her glory.'

For thus says the Lord:

'Behold, I will extend peace to her like a river,
And the glory of the Gentiles like a flowing stream.
Then you shall feed;
On her sides shall you be carried,
And be dandled on her knees.
As one whom his mother comforts,
So will I comfort you;
And you shall be comforted in Jerusalem.'

Day 27
Rejoicing with Jerusalem

♦ *Begin by reading Isaiah 66*
♦ *Pray about what you have read*
♦ *Make notes on what you think God is teaching you*
♦ *Read the following chapter*
♦ *Answer the questions in the section 'For your journal'*

Isaiah 66:10-13

We have been reminding ourselves throughout this series that the last twenty-seven chapters of Isaiah were truly prophetic in nature. The prophet was enabled by the Spirit of God to see the future of his people. We can divide that future into two parts. The immediate future would be most distressing indeed. It would involve seventy long years of captivity in Babylon. But the more distant future would be as blessed and glorious as the immediate would be unpleasant.

The verses of our text point the people towards that bright future. In these verses the Lord commands his people to rejoice with Jerusalem. Here is an astonishing thing: Jerusalem would lie in ruins for the seventy years of the captivity, but God commands his people to rejoice with her. The captives had to understand that to mean that devastation was not the final word for Jerusalem. God was planning wonderful things for her.

All of this will seem to have little or no meaning for us unless we associate Jerusalem with the church. When we do so, this passage begins to brim with vitality. It also has some very pointed applications for us.

Our attitude towards the church

We should note that the Lord addressed this command to those who loved Jerusalem and mourned for her (v. 10). It is very difficult for us to fully understand what Jerusalem meant to the captives in Babylon and how often they thought of her. One of the psalmists conveyed something of this in these words:

> By the rivers of Babylon,
> There we sat down, yea, we wept
> When we remembered Zion.
>
> …
>
> If I forget you, O Jerusalem,
> Let my right hand forget its skill!
> If I do not remember you,
> Let my tongue cling to the roof of my mouth —
> If I do not exalt Jerusalem
> Above my chief joy

(Ps. 137:1, 5-6).

We will be hard pressed to explain such attachment to Jerusalem unless we remember that she was far more than a place to the captives. Jerusalem represented unspeakably wonderful truths to them. She was the very centre of their religious life. Her very presence meant that God had revealed himself to the people of Israel. It meant that God had delivered them from bondage and brought them into a covenant relationship with himself. It represented God's blessings upon the nation, and the hope of the Messiah. All of this and much more was bound up in the name Jerusalem. That city represented the very essence of true religion.

To love Jerusalem was, in a sense, to love true religion. And to mourn for her was to mourn the losses sustained by true religion. Can we relate to how these people felt about their city? The church should mean as much, and more, to us as Jerusalem did to those people. Do we fervently love the church? Do we desire to see her prosper? Do we delight in the truth she represents? Are we saddened when she declines?

I love thy kingdom, Lord, the house of thine abode,
The church our blest Redeemer saved with his own precious blood.

I love thy church, O God: her walls before thee stand,
Dear as the apple of thine eye, and graven on thy hand.

For her my tears shall fall, for her my prayers ascend;
To her my cares and toils be giv'n, till toils and cares shall end.

Beyond the highest joy I prize her heav'nly ways,
Her sweet communion, solemn vows, her hymns of love and
*   praise.*
*   Timothy Dwight, 'I Love Thy Kingdom, Lord'*

Reasons for rejoicing in the church

The captives who mourned for Jerusalem while they were in Babylon would see their mourning turned to joy. What would be the cause of this great change? God was going to do marvellous things for the city of Jerusalem.

Some of those things are laid out here in our text. God would make Jerusalem a place of satisfying food and delightful drink (v. 11). He would give Jerusalem constant and abundant peace (v. 12). He would make the city attractive to others (v. 12). He would use her to bring comfort to his people (vv. 12-13).

All of these details find parallels in the church, and all of these parallels are reasons for rejoicing.

The church is a place of satisfying food and delightful drink

The Lord promised the captives that they would rejoice with Jerusalem because they would there 'feed and be satisfied' and 'drink deeply and be delighted' (v. 11).

David found a fulness in the house of the Lord, which he celebrated by speaking these words to the Lord:

> ...the children of men ...
> are abundantly satisfied with the fulness of your house,
> And you give them drink from the river of your pleasures
> (Ps. 36:7-8).

The food which satisfies the church is the Word of God. This leads us immediately to two very important observations. One of these pertains to the pastor. When the people of God gather, it is his solemn responsibility to put before them food that will satisfy. Many are failing to do this. They offer substitutes for the Word of God and the people leave unsatisfied.

The other observation pertains to the people. Just as the pastor is under solemn obligation to feed his people the satisfying Word of God, so the people are under the solemn obligation to come and hear. One who professes faith in Christ and habitually stays away from the preaching of God's Word is horribly deceived about his spiritual condition.

The delightful drink of the church is 'the abundance of her glory' (v. 11). The church has a glory about her. How very hard it is for those who are familiar with her to see this! When Jesus was on the Mount of Transfiguration, the disciples who were with him — Peter, James and John — slept. But Luke tells us 'when they were fully awake, they saw his glory' (Luke 9:32).

We need to wake up so we can see the glory of the church. That glory consists of several things. The church's glory is in the Lord who came and died for her to make her his own. It is in the Lord who meets with his people when they gather in his name. It is in the worship that exalts his name. It is in the care the members have for each other. It is in the glorious future that awaits the church.

Each and every Sunday we are to gather together to eat the satisfying food of God's Word and to drink in the delightful glories of the church.

The church is a place of peace

In our text the Lord says of Jerusalem, 'I will extend peace to her like a river...' (v. 12). Jerusalem had known very little peace for a very long time. The Babylonians had come in and devastated her. But all that would change, and Jerusalem's peace would flow constantly and abundantly like the water of a river.

We should rejoice in the peace of the church. She consists of those who are at peace with God. They were once the enemies of God, but, through his saving power, they have been reconciled to him. The church is also to consist of people who are at peace with each other. We cannot claim peace with God if we are at war with each other.

The church is attractive to others

God promised the captives in Babylon that the Gentiles would come flowing into Jerusalem (v. 12). He was going to make her such an attractive place that outsiders would desire to come and be a part of her. This promise finds its fulfilment in Gentiles flowing into the church. How abundant this fulfilment has been! God has flung the doors of his church wide open to the Gentiles, and they have poured in to the praise of his grace. Jesus himself foretold the ingathering of the Gentiles with these words: 'And other sheep I have which are not of this fold; them also I must bring, and they will hear my voice; and there will be one flock and one shepherd' (John 10:16).

We should be thankful for the note of certainty in these words. The Lord Jesus does not say that he would *try* to gather his other sheep (the Gentiles), but rather that he *would* gather them. Their coming to him was so certain that he could affirm that they would hear his voice and be part of his flock. It was certain because these sheep already belonged to him, having been chosen by the Father and given to the Son before the foundation of the world (Eph. 1:3-6).

This work of ingathering still goes on, and it will not stop until all those chosen by the Father and redeemed by the Son are safely home in heaven.

This gives us great encouragement regarding the present work of the church. It may often appear to us that the church is very weak and feeble and that she is failing in her work. Let us always remember that it is the Lord Jesus himself who promised to so build his church that the very gates of hell would not be able to prevail against her (Matt. 16:18).

No matter how feverishly Satan works, he will not be able to thwart the plan and purpose of God. On the basis of this reality, disheartened believers can even now look forward to the vast number of converts the Lord will yet bring into his church as she continues to delight herself in God and to enjoy his peace.

The church comforts her people

What tender language the Lord uses to describe how Jerusalem would bring comfort to her citizens! He says:

> 'On her sides shall you be carried,
> And be dandled on her knees.
> As one whom his mother comforts,
> So I will comfort you;
> And you shall be comforted in Jerusalem'
>
> (vv. 12-13).

We understand the word 'dandle' as meaning to dance an infant up and down on the knee. It is an expression of affectionate tenderness. The parent may very well begin this 'dandling' when the infant is half-asleep, sluggish or slightly out of sorts. Soon the baby is wide awake and smiling.

How very often God has used the church to dandle us! The cares and burdens of life can cause us to come into her doors half-asleep or feeling sluggish and unhappy. But we were not there long before we found the Lord 'dandling' us, that is, using the services and the fellowship of the church to make us aware of how much he loves us and how much his church means to him. And we leave feeling thrilled that we are part of it all.

Just as the ancient captives who loved Jerusalem would have many reasons to rejoice in her, so we who love the church have many reasons to rejoice too. May God help us to do so.

For your journal...

1. Write a paragraph about what the church means to you. Look at what you have written. Spend some time thanking God for the church.

2. Can you think of times when you went to church feeling very low and found yourself being 'dandled' by God, that is, made aware of his love and affection for you? Select one of these experiences and write a paragraph or two about it.

Notes

Day 1 – Our deliverer and shepherd
1. Matthew Henry, *Matthew Henry's Commentary*, Fleming H. Revell Publishing Co., vol. iv, p.211.
2. Albert Barnes, *Notes on the Old Testament: Isaiah II*, Baker Book House, p.64.
3. Reformation Heritage Books, p.19.

Day 2 – Unbreakable cords of comfort
1. Barnes, *Notes*, p.86.
2. Alan Redpath, *Faith for the Times*, Fleming H. Revell Publishing Co., vol. i, pp.35-6.

Day 3 – The comforting Christ
1. Barnes, *Notes*, p.98.
2. As above, p.102.
3. Derek Thomas, *God Delivers*, Evangelical Press, p.281.
4. Henry, *Commentary*, vol. iv, p.228.

Day 4 – The flood and the furnace
1. Redpath, *Faith for the Times*, p.65.

Day 5 – The devotions of God
1. InterVarsity Press, pp.104-5.

Day 6 – A gracious invitation and a solemn warning
1. Evangelical Press, vol. ii, p.109.

Day 7 – Three unfailing things
1. Cited by Thomas, *God Delivers*, p.313.
2. Baker Book House, pp.169-70.

Day 8 – Double comfort
1. Baker Book House, p.176.

Day 9 – Setting the record straight
1. Barnes, *Notes*, p.193.
2. Fleming H. Revell Company, vol. iv, p.274.

Day 10 – For those who feel forgotten by God
1. Alexander Maclaren, *Expositions of Holy Scripture*, Baker Book House, vol. v, p.9.
2. As above, p.12.
3. Fleming H. Revell Company, vol. ii, p.17.

Day 11 – Hallelujah! What a Saviour!
1. William Hendriksen, *New Testament Commentary: John*, Baker Book House, p.414.
2. Barnes, *Notes*, p.221.
3. As above, p.222.
4. Fleming H. Revell Company, vol. iv, p.287.

Day 13 – The joyous reception of a joyous proclamation
1. The Banner of Truth Trust, vol. i, p.559.

Day 14 – An amazingly detailed preview of Christ
1. The Banner of Truth Trust, vol. i, p.560.

Day 15 – The immovable and the unproductive
1. Baker Book House, pp.295-6.
2. Barnes, *Notes*, p.296.

Day 16 – Abundant pardon
1. Thomas, *God Delivers*, p.347.
2. Tanski Publications, vol. iii, p.415.

Day 17 – Our gathering God
1. The Banner of Truth Trust, vol. xxix, p.187.
2. Henry, *Commentary*, p.323.

Day 18 – Reasons to believe and not doubt
1. Henry, *Commentary*, p.332.
2. Tanski Publications, vol. iii, p.420.
3. As above.

Day 19 – A promise of blessing and the pathway to blessing
1. Henry, *Commentary*, p.340.
2. As above, pp.340-1.
3. Barnes, *Notes*, p.335.

Day 20 – What God saw; what God did
1. Barnes, *Notes*, p.351.
2. As above.

Day 21 – A new day and an endless day
1. Barnes, *Notes*, p.369.
2. Thomas, *God Delivers*, p.366.
3. Evangelical Press, p.216.

Day 22 – Life's supreme blessing
1. John Gill, *Exposition of the Old & New Testaments*, The Baptist Standard Bearer, vol. v, p.362.

Day 23 – Hephzibah: God's delight in his people
1. The Banner of Truth Trust, p.108.

Day 24 – What to mention in times of trouble
1. The Banner of Truth Trust, vol. i, p.294.
2. Henry, *Commentary*, vol. iv, p.370.

Day 25 – A prayer for revival
1. Jonathan Edwards, *The Works of Jonathan Edwards*, The Banner of Truth Trust, vol. i, p.426.
2. As above.
3. Fleming H. Revell Company, vol. iv, p.378.

Day 26 – Good things to know about God
1. The Baptist Standard Bearer, Inc., vol. v, p.386.

Notes...

Notes...

Notes...

Notes...

Notes...

Notes...

More from the author…

THE BIBLE BOOK BY BOOK

The Bible book by book is the first in a new series of publications called *The Guide*. This book provides a complete overview of the Bible, divided into fifty-two chapters, which is ideal for use as a resource for a group Bible study or on an individual basis. It covers every book of the Bible, giving both its historical and spiritual significance, and shows how each individual book fits into God's perfect plan for his people throughout history.

The aim of *The Guide* series is to communicate the Christian faith in a straightforward and readable way, and to that end each chapter is relatively short and concise. An innovative feature of the series is that it is linked to its own web site, which can be found at www.evangelicalpress.org, where further questions may be posted, to be answered by a team of experienced, dedicated men.

The Bible book by book, Roger Ellsworth, ISBN 0 85234 486 4, 432 pages, Evangelical Press.

Be patient, God hasn't finished with me yet!

Jacob lived a very long time ago. There were no computers. Jacob did not send or receive E-mail. There were no television sets, no VCRs, and no cars. What possible value is there, then, in studying the life of a man so far removed from our own sophisticated times?

Simply because Jacob is a picture of us all. We all come into this world with a nature that makes us oblivious to the things of God and engrossed in ourselves. Even those of us who have become Christians are never free from struggle against sin in this life.

In this book, Roger Ellsworth shows us what a hard struggle it was for Jacob. It is apparent that he was a deeply flawed man, completely wrapped up in himself and willing to trample on those around him, even his own family, to achieve his selfish ends.

Yet what an immensely blessed man Jacob was! The Lord had chosen his grandfather Abraham to be the father of the nation of Israel, and Jacob was, by God's grace, the one who was to receive the blessing of God's promises. Left to himself, Jacob would have been a blot on the pages of history; but God had other plans. His grace is greater than Jacob's sin!

Be patient, God hasn't finished with me yet!, Roger Ellsworth, ISBN 0 85234 524 0, 128 pages, Evangelical Press.

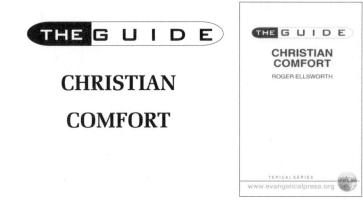

THE GUIDE

CHRISTIAN
COMFORT

The Christian life is rarely trouble-free and there are many trials that the people of God have to go through. They frequently need comfort and can even become despondent as they seek to cope with personal trials and afflictions, and as they face the abounding wickedness and ever-increasing hostility of a godless world.

In this book in *The Guide* series Roger Ellsworth shows that the greatest comfort comes from God himself, who is indeed the source of all comfort. He is the one who can alleviate grief and encourage believers during the deepest of trials. There is no situation in which he cannot bring his comfort, and when we have experienced his love and care during such times we are encouraged to comfort others, until that coming day when we will sorrow no more because we are with him in eternity.

'In a series of short, snappy chapters, Roger Ellsworth has helpfully set out a biblical response for virtually every situation and condition requiring comfort … He is clear, direct and challenging. A useful guide for those times when things seem to be going wrong.'

Rev. Daniel Webber
Mission Director, European Missionary Fellowship

Christian comfort, Roger Ellsworth, ISBN 0 85234 540 2, 240 pages, Evangelical Press.

A wide range of excellent books on spiritual subjects is available from Evangelical Press. Please write to us for your free catalogue or contact us by e-mail.

Evangelical Press
Faverdale North Industrial Estate, Darlington, DL3 0PH, England

Evangelical Press USA
P. O. Box 825, Webster, New York 14580, USA

e-mail: sales@evangelicalpress.org
web: www.evangelicalpress.org